GoodFood
Easy weeknight
suppers

10 9 8 7 6 5 4 3 2 1

Published in 2012 by BBC Books, an imprint of Ebury Publishing.
A Random House Group Company

The Random House Group Limited
Reg. No. 954009

Addresses for companies within th[e Random House Group can be found at:]
www.randomhouse.co.uk

A CIP catalogue record for this boo[k is available from the British Library.]

The Random House Group Limited [supports The Forest Stewardship Council ® (FSC ®), the leading
international forest certification org[anisation. All our titles that] are printed on FSC® certified
paper. FSC is the only forest certific[ation scheme endorsed by the leading environmental organisations,]
including Greenpeace. Our paper pr[ocurement policy can be found at www.randomhouse.co.uk/environment.]

To buy books by your favourite auth[ors and register for offers visit www.randomhouse.co.uk.]

Printed and bound by Firmengrupp[e ...]

Commissioning editor: Muna Reyal
Project editor: Sarah Watling
Designer: Kathryn Gammon
Production: Phil Spencer
Picture researcher: Gabby Harringto[n]

ISBN: 9781849905312

Picture credits

BBC *Good Food* magazine would like to thank the following people for providing photos. While every effort has been made
to trace and acknowledge all photographers we should like to apologise should there be any errors or omissions.

Peter Cassidy p25, p29, p69; Will Heap p45, p49, p57, p77, p83, p89, p103, p133, p145, p159, p163, p211; Sian Irvine p143,
p153, p173; Gareth Morgans p183, p191, p203; David Munns p11, p17, p19, p61, p67, p73, p75, p79, p81, p87, p91, p95, p97,
p99, p115, p117, p119, p121, p123, 125, p127, 135, p155, p157, p169, p175, p177, p179, p193, p201; Myles New p113; Stuart
Ovenden p13, p15, p21, p33, p37, p39, p41, p43, p63, p65, p105, p187; Lis Parsons p31, p71, p101, p107, p109, p111, p141,
p181, p185, p205, p207; Charlie Richards p93, p137, p139, p147, p167, p171; Simon Smith p35; Yuki Sugiura p23, p47, p51,
p55, p59, p129, p131, p161, p165, p195; Jon Whitaker p27, p53, p189; Isobel Wield p197

All the recipes in this book were created by the editorial team at *Good Food* and by regular contributors to BBC magazines.

easy

GoodFood
Easy weeknight suppers

Editor **Barney Desmazery**

BOOKS

Contents

Introduction

Coming up with something new and inspiring to eat on a weeknight can be a challenge for even the most experienced of cooks, but now there's no need to worry because this little book has 101 answers for that dilemma.

At *Good Food* we are experts at devising meal solutions, and for this weeknight collection we've combined our favourite recipes that are quick to prepare, easy to follow and, like all our recipes, have been tested in our kitchens so we know they work first time.

The variety of ingredients now available to us in supermarkets has really grown in the last few years, so we've used that to our advantage and in this book you'll find a good balance of modern recipes alongside the firm family favourites that we all turn to for a bit of familiar comfort.

Eating healthily on weeknights is something that we all know we should be doing, so we've included recipes that have something to add to a healthy diet, be it recipes that contain lots of vegetables or ones that are low in fat, sugar or salt, or are simply good for you.

So now there is no excuse to be stuck in a weeknight meal rut, with this book by your side you will always have an answer to that daily question: what's for supper?

Barney

Notes and conversion tables

NOTES ON THE RECIPES
- Eggs are large in the UK and Australia and extra large in America unless stated otherwise.
- Wash fresh produce before preparation.
- Recipes contain nutritional analyses for 'sugar', which means the total sugar content including all natural sugars in the ingredients, unless otherwise stated.

OVEN TEMPERATURES

Gas	°C	°C Fan	°F	Oven temp.
¼	110	90	225	Very cool
½	120	100	250	Very cool
1	140	120	275	Cool or slow
2	150	130	300	Cool or slow
3	160	140	325	Warm
4	180	160	350	Moderate
5	190	170	375	Moderately hot
6	200	180	400	Fairly hot
7	220	200	425	Hot
8	230	210	450	Very hot
9	240	220	475	Very hot

APPROXIMATE WEIGHT CONVERSIONS
- All the recipes in this book list both imperial and metric measurements. Conversions are approximate and have been rounded up or down. Follow one set of measurements only; do not mix the two.
- Cup measurements, which are used by cooks in Australia and America, have not been listed here as they vary from ingredient to ingredient. Kitchen scales should be used to measure dry/solid ingredients.

Good Food is concerned about sustainable sourcing and animal welfare. Where possible humanely reared meats, sustainably caught fish (see fishonline. org for further information from the Marine Conservation Society) and free-range chickens and eggs are used when recipes are originally tested.

SPOON MEASURES

Spoon measurements are level unless otherwise specified.

- 1 teaspoon (tsp) = 5ml
- 1 tablespoon (tbsp) = 15ml
- 1 Australian tablespoon = 20ml (cooks in Australia should measure 3 teaspoons where 1 tablespoon is specified in a recipe)

APPROXIMATE LIQUID CONVERSIONS

metric	imperial	AUS	US
50ml	2fl oz	¼ cup	¼ cup
125ml	4fl oz	½ cup	½ cup
175ml	6fl oz	¾ cup	¾ cup
225ml	8fl oz	1 cup	1 cup
300ml	10fl oz/½ pint	½ pint	1¼ cups
450ml	16fl oz	2 cups	2 cups/1 pint
600ml	20fl oz/1 pint	1 pint	2½ cups
1 litre	35fl oz/1¾ pints	1¾ pints	1 quart

Creamy lentil & spinach soup with bacon

This filling main-meal soup can easily be made vegetarian by omitting the bacon at the end.

TAKES 1 HOUR • SERVES 4

2 tbsp olive oil, plus extra for frying
2 onions, finely chopped
2 carrots, finely chopped
2 celery sticks, finely chopped
140g/5oz green lentils
1.5 litres/2¾ pints weak vegetable
    stock
200g bag baby leaf spinach
4 tbsp double cream, plus a drizzle
    to garnish
6 rashers smoked streaky bacon

1 Put the oil, onions, carrots and celery in a large pan, and cook for about 10 minutes to soften.

2 Stir in the lentils and pour in the stock. Bring to the boil, then turn down and simmer for 30–35 minutes or until the lentils are soft, topping up with water if the mixture begins to dry out. Pop in the spinach and cook for a few minutes more, until wilted. With a hand blender or in a food processor blitz the soup until smooth, then stir through the cream and season.

3 Heat a little oil in a non-stick pan over a medium heat. Add the bacon and fry until crisp and golden. Reheat the soup and ladle into bowls, drizzle with a little extra cream and crumble over the crispy bacon.

PER SERVING 479 kcals, protein 18g, carbs 29g, fat 32g, sat fat 14g, fibre 8g, sugar 12g, salt 2.2g

Courgette, feta & mint salad

This quick no-cook salad delivers maximum flavour with minimal effort.

TAKES 10 MINUTES • SERVES 4

2 courgettes
100g bag rocket leaves
200g pack feta, crumbled
bunch mint, leaves picked
your favourite dressing, to drizzle

1 Slice the courgettes into long ribbons with a potato peeler.
2 Scatter the rocket over a large platter then scatter over the courgettes. Crumble over the feta and mint leaves, and drizzle on your favourite dressing.

PER SERVING 152 kcals, protein 10g, carbs 3.5g, fat 11g, sat fat 7g, fibre 1g, sugar 2.5g, salt 1.9g

Hot & sour seafood fish soup

Even though this sounds exotic there is nothing in this recipe that you won't be able to find in most large supermarkets.

TAKES 45 MINUTES • SERVES 4

1 tsp coriander seeds
small piece ginger, sliced
850ml/1½ pints fish or chicken stock
175g/6oz thin rice noodles
2 tbsp fish sauce
2 red chillies, deseeded and thinly
 sliced
3 garlic cloves, thinly sliced
300g/10oz raw tiger prawns
200g/7oz skinless salmon fillet, cut into
 small cubes
4 spring onions, chopped
handful coriander leaves and handful
 mint leaves, torn
juice 2 limes

1 Put the coriander seeds and ginger in a pan. Pour in the stock, bring to the boil, then simmer gently for 5 minutes. Leave to stand for 10 minutes.
2 Meanwhile, cook the noodles according to the pack instructions and drain.
3 Return the stock to the boil. Add the fish sauce, chillies and garlic, reduce the heat and simmer for 2 minutes. Add the prawns and salmon, return to a simmer and cook gently for about 5 minutes until both are firm and cooked. Add the spring onions, herbs and lime juice, to taste.
4 Divide the noodles among four soup bowls. Using a slotted spoon, lift out the prawns and fish, and put them on top of the noodles. Season the hot stock, then pour into the bowls and serve.

PER SERVING 322 kcals, protein 29g, carbs 39g, fat 7g, sat fat 1g, fibre 1g, sugar 1g, salt 3.46g

Cobb salad with buttermilk ranch dressing

If you can't find buttermilk for the dressing then soured cream or natural yogurt would be fine too.

TAKES 15 MINUTES • SERVES 2

2 Baby Gem lettuces, leaves separated

1 avocado, stoned and sliced

2 plum tomatoes, chopped

3 rashers cooked crispy bacon

140g/5oz cooked turkey breast or
  chicken, cut into bite-sized pieces

2 hard-boiled eggs, chopped into
  chunks

FOR THE DRESSING

75ml/2½fl oz buttermilk

2 tbsp light mayonnaise

1 tbsp white wine vinegar

1 tbsp chopped dill

½ garlic clove, crushed

1 In a small bowl, whisk the dressing ingredients together with some salt until completely combined and set aside.

2 Neatly arrange the salad ingredients separately on two plates or one large platter to share, and serve with the dressing on the side.

PER SERVING 472 kcals, protein 43g, carbs 8g, fat 30g, sat fat 8g, fibre 4g, sugar 7g, salt 2.5g

Caramelised onion & barley soup with cheese croutons

This classic onion soup is made all the more wholesome with the clever addition of nutritiously filling barley.

TAKES 45 MINUTES ● **SERVES 2**

1 tbsp olive oil

2 medium onions, thinly sliced

2 garlic cloves, thinly sliced

6 thyme sprigs, chopped

good pinch sugar

500ml/18fl oz vegetable stock

60g/2½oz barley

60g/2½oz kale, thick stalks discarded and leaves sliced

4 slices baguette, toasted

4 tbsp grated cheese, like Gruyère or Cheddar

1 Heat the oil in a pan, then add the onions, garlic, thyme, sugar and a good pinch of salt. Cook on a medium – low heat for 15–20 minutes or until golden. Add the stock and simmer for a further 10 minutes.

2 In a separate large pan of salted boiling water, cook the barley for 15 minutes, adding the kale for the final 3 minutes of cooking. Drain and rinse under cold water, then add to the soup and warm through.

3 Heat the grill. Top the toasted bread with cheese and put under the grill until it's bubbly and melted. Serve the soup in two large bowls with the cheesy croutons on top.

PER SERVING 434 kcals, protein 15g, carbs 59g, fat 15g, sat fat 5g, fibre 6g, sugar 13g, salt 1.4g

Bean, ham & egg salad

A chunky salad you can add any of your other favourite salad ingredients to – cherry tomatoes would work nicely.

TAKES 30 MINUTES • SERVES 4

2 hard-boiled eggs
500g/1lb 2oz baby potatoes
200g/7oz green beans
200g/7oz frozen peas, defrosted
175g/6oz lean ham, shredded
crusty bread, to serve (optional)

FOR THE DRESSING

juice ½ lemon
1 tbsp wholegrain mustard
1 tbsp clear honey

1 Peel and quarter the eggs. Cook the potatoes in a large pan of boiling water for 8–10 minutes or until tender. Tip in the beans for the final 3 minutes, then add the peas for the final minute. Drain all the veg, cool under cold running water, then drain again really well.

2 For the dressing, mix the lemon juice, mustard and honey together in a small bowl. Season, then pour over the vegetables. Fold through the ham and top with the eggs. Serve with bread, if you like.

PER SERVING 240 kcals, protein 17g, carbs 29g, fat 6g, sat fat 2g, fibre 5g, sugar 9g, salt 1.6g

Spiced turkey with bulghar & pomegranate salad

This salad is not only low fat, fresh, light and healthy but also surprisingly substantial and filling.

TAKES 40 MINUTES • SERVES 4

2 tbsp each chopped dill, parsley and mint

zest and juice 1 lemon

1 tbsp harissa paste

500g/1lb 2oz turkey breast fillets

2 tbsp white wine or water

250g pack bulghar wheat or a mix (we used quinoa and bulghar mix)

2 tomatoes, chopped

½ cucumber, diced

100g pack pomegranate seeds

1 Heat oven to 200C/180C fan/gas 6. Mix together half the herbs, half the lemon zest and juice, and all the harissa with some seasoning. Rub the turkey in the marinade and leave for 5 minutes (or up to 24 hours in the fridge).

2 Lay out a large sheet of foil. Put the turkey and marinade, and wine or water, on top, then cover with another layer of foil, fold and crimp the edges to seal. Transfer the parcel to a baking sheet, then bake for 30 minutes until cooked through.

3 Meanwhile, make the salad. Cook the bulghar according to the pack instructions. Drain, then mix with the remaining herbs, lemon zest and juice, plus the tomatoes, cucumber and pomegranate seeds.

4 Slice the turkey and serve on top of the salad with the juices from the foil parcel poured on top.

PER SERVING 304 kcals, protein 41g, carbs 23g, fat 9g, sat fat 1g, fibre 4g, sugar 7g, salt 0.7g

Crunchy cauliflower, apple & blue cheese salad

The combination of crunchy cauliflower, crisp apple with creamy, salty blue cheese is a total winner.

TAKES 15 MINUTES • SERVES 4

3–4 apples, cored, halved and sliced
1 small cauliflower, cut into florettes
handful alfalfa sprouts (optional)
200g/7oz Stilton or vegetarian crumbly
    blue cheese, such as Dorset Blue
    Vinny, crumbled
small bunch mint, chopped
50g/2oz sunflower seeds, toasted
FOR THE DRESSING
5 tbsp cider vinegar
2 tbsp extra virgin olive or rapeseed oil
little drizzle of clear honey

1 Make the dressing by whisking the vinegar, oil and honey with some seasoning.
2 Pour the dressing over the sliced apples then gently mix in the cauliflower, alfalfa sprouts (if using) and cheese. Scatter over the mint and the toasted seeds just before serving.

PER SERVING 417 kcals, protein 19g, carbs 18g, fat 30g, sat fat 13g, fibre 5g, sugar 15g, salt 1.05g

Prawn salad with orange, red onion & avocado

This no-cook supper for two is just the thing for a warm summer evening when you really don't want to turn on the stove.

TAKES 10 MINUTES ● SERVES 2

2 oranges
1 Little Gem lettuce, leaves separated
1 ripe avocado
140g/5oz cooked king prawns, peeled
1 small red onion, finely sliced
small bunch coriander, leaves picked
2 tbsp sweet chilli dipping sauce
juice ½ lime

1 Stand each orange on a board and cut away the peel and pith with a sharp knife. Cut the oranges into 1cm/ ½in slices and set aside.

2 Arrange the lettuce on two plates, halve, stone and peel the avocado, then slice. Put the avocado on top of the lettuce leaves and scatter the prawns on top.

3 Divide the orange slices, onion and coriander leaves between each plate and toss together very lightly.

4 For the dressing, mix the dipping sauce and lime juice together in a small bowl and season with black pepper. Spoon over the salad and serve.

PER SERVING 259 kcals, protein 14g, carbs 17g, fat 15g, sat fat 3g, fibre 5g, sugar 15g, salt 1.7g

Griddled chicken & corn on the cob salad

Weather and time permitting, this recipe can be easily adapted for a little midweek barbecue.

TAKES 30 MINUTES • SERVES 4

4 small skinless chicken breasts
2 garlic cloves, crushed
1 tbsp paprika
juice 1 lemon
2 tbsp olive oil
2 corn cobs
4 Baby Gem lettuces, quartered
  lengthways
½ cucumber, diced
your favourite dressing, to drizzle

1 Cut the chicken breasts in half lengthways so you are left with eight thinner chicken pieces. Mix the garlic, paprika, lemon juice and 1 tablespoon of the oil with some seasoning and toss with chicken. Marinate for at least 15 minutes.

2 Brush a griddle pan with half the remaining oil and cook the chicken for 3–4 minutes each side, until cooked through. Heat the remaining oil and griddle the corn cobs until lightly charred, about 5 minutes, turning to cook evenly. Remove and cut off the kernels.

3 Mix the leaves and cucumber, top with the corn kernels and chicken, and drizzle with your favourite dressing.

PER SERVING 236 kcals, protein 28g, carbs 12g, fat 8g, sat fat 1.3g, fibre 3g, sugar 3.7g, salt 0.2g

Smoked haddock & white bean soup

If you have some saffron you can use it instead of the turmeric – it will give the soup a beautiful yellow colour.

TAKES 40 MINUTES • SERVES 6

50g/2oz butter

2 large onions, thinly sliced

400g can cannellini beans, rinsed and drained

500ml/18fl oz chicken stock

270ml pot whipping cream

¼ tsp ground turmeric

½ tsp mild curry powder

450g/1lb undyed smoked haddock fillets, skinned

snipped chives, to garnish (optional)

1 Heat the butter in a non-stick pan. Add the onions and fry very gently for 15 minutes until soft but not coloured. Stir in the beans, chicken stock, cream and the turmeric and curry powder, then cover and cook gently for 5 minutes.

2 Add the haddock fillets, then cover and cook for 5–8 minutes more until the fish is just cooked and flakes when tested.

3 Take out one-third of the haddock and set aside, then blitz the soup in the pan with a hand blender, or blend in a food processor until smooth. Add the flaked fish to the pan and reheat gently. To serve, ladle into bowls and scatter with the snipped chives, if you like.

PER SERVING 375 kcals, protein 22g, carbs 14g, fat 26g, sat fat 16g, fibre 3g, sugar 6g, salt 1.97g

Spinach, bacon & white bean salad

A sweet honey-based dressing works best with the saltiness of the bacon in this salad.

TAKES 20 MINUTES SERVES 4

12 rashers smoked streaky bacon
4 tbsp sherry vinegar
2 × 280g jar roasted red peppers, drained and sliced
2 × 400g cans borlotti beans, rinsed and drained
150g bag baby spinach leaves
your favourite dressing, to serve

1 Heat a large pan and dry-fry the bacon until crispy, about 2 minutes each side, then remove and drain on kitchen paper. Keep the fat from the bacon in the pan then add the vinegar and bubble for a few seconds before tipping in the peppers and beans. Season and heat through.
2 Toss the spinach, beans, peppers and bacon together in a large serving bowl, then scatter over a platter and drizzle with a dressing of your choice.

PER SERVING 300 kcals, protein 21g, carbs 19g, fat 15g, sat fat 5g, fibre 8.6g, sugar 1g, salt 2.1g

Broccoli & Stilton soup

A smooth, blended vegetable soup with blue cheese that's as good for a comforting weeknight meal as it is for a weekend dinner-party starter.

TAKES 45 MINUTES • SERVES 4

2 tbsp rapeseed oil
1 onion, finely chopped
1 celery stick, sliced
1 leek, sliced
1 medium potato, diced
knob butter
1 litre/1¾ pints low-salt or homemade chicken or vegetable stock
1 head broccoli, stalk and head separated, both roughly chopped
140g/4oz Stilton or other blue cheese, crumbled

1 Heat the oil in a large pan with a lid and then add the onion. Cook on a medium heat until soft. Add a splash of water if the onion starts to catch.
2 Add the celery, leek, potato and butter. Stir until melted, then cover with a lid. Allow to sweat for 5 minutes. Remove the lid.
3 Pour in the stock and add any chunky bits of broccoli stalk. Cook for 10–15 minutes until all the vegetables are soft. Add the rest of the broccoli and cook for a further 5 minutes. Using a hand blender, blitz until smooth. Stir in the cheese, allowing a few lumps to remain. Season with black pepper and serve.

PER SERVING 340 kcals, protein 24.3g, carbs 14g, fat 21g, sat fat 9.6g, fibre 7g, sugar 5g, salt 1.4g

Mexican salad with tortilla croutons

To make this salad even easier you could use ready-made tortilla chips rather than making the croutons.

TAKES 20 MINUTES • SERVES 4

3 flour tortillas, cut into crouton-sized pieces

1 tbsp olive oil

1 tsp Cajun or Mexican seasoning mix

1 iceberg lettuce, shredded

400g can black beans, rinsed and drained

200g pack cherry tomatoes, halved

2 avocados, halved, stoned and sliced

juice 1 lime

your favourite dressing, to drizzle

½ bunch coriander, leaves only, to garnish

1 Heat oven to 200C/180C fan/gas 6. Put the tortilla strips on a baking sheet, toss with the oil and spicy seasoning, and cook for 10–12 minutes, until crisp.

2 In a large bowl toss together the lettuce, beans and cherry tomatoes. Combine the avocados and lime juice, and add the mix to the bowl too.

3 Drizzle over your preferred dressing and toss to coat all the ingredients. Top with the croutons and coriander leaves before serving.

PER SERVING 337 kcals, protein 11g, carbs 42g, fat 14g, sat fat 3g, fibre 9g, sugar 5g, salt 0.4g

Curried squash, lentil & coconut soup

It's worth making more of this soup than you need as it keeps well and can be taken to work and easily reheated in a microwave.

TAKES 25 MINUTES • SERVES 6

1 tbsp olive oil

1 butternut squash, peeled, deseeded
   and diced

200g/7oz carrots, diced

1 tbsp curry powder containing
   turmeric

100g/4oz red split lentils

700ml/1¼ pints vegetable stock

1 can reduced-fat coconut milk

chopped coriander leaves, to garnish

naan bread, to serve

1 Heat the oil in a large pan, add the squash and carrots, sizzle for 1 minute, then stir in the curry powder and cook for 1 minute more. Tip in the lentils, vegetable stock and coconut milk, and give everything a good stir. Bring to the boil, then turn the heat down and simmer for 15–18 minutes until everything is tender.

2 Using a hand-held blender or a food processor, blitz until as smooth as you like. Season and serve scattered with roughly chopped coriander and some naan bread alongside.

PER SERVING 178 kcals, protein 6g, carbs 22g, fat 7g, sat fat 5g, fibre 4g, sugar 9g, salt 0.4g

Spiced cauliflower with chickpeas, herbs & pine nuts

This superhealthy main-meal salad also makes a brilliant all-in-one side dish for grilled lamb chops.

TAKES 50 MINUTES • SERVES 4

1 cauliflower, broken into florets (about 1kg/2lb 4oz total)
2 fat garlic cloves, crushed
2 tsp each caraway and cumin seeds
3 tbsp olive oil
400g can chickpeas, rinsed and drained
100g/4oz pine nuts
small bunch each parsley and dill, leaves torn
your favourite dressing, to drizzle

1 Heat oven to 200C/180C fan/gas 6. In a roasting tin, toss the cauliflower with the garlic and spices, 2 tablespoons of the oil and some seasoning, then roast for 30 minutes until golden and tender.

2 After 30 minutes, add the chickpeas and pine nuts to the tin with the rest of the oil. Return to the oven for 10 minutes more. Finally, stir in the herbs with your chosen dressing and serve.

PER SERVING 407 kcals, protein 17g, carbs 19g, fat 29g, sat fat 3g, fibre 10g, sugar 7g, salt 0.5g

Tomato & onion bake with goat's cheese

This saucy gratin needs to be served with crusty bread to mop up all the delicious juices.

TAKES 50 MINUTES • SERVES 4

6 onions, halved (keep root intact)
4 garlic cloves, finely sliced
2 tbsp olive oil
2 × 400g cans chopped tomatoes
1 tsp caster sugar
85g/3oz white breadcrumbs
125g log goat's cheese, crumbled

1 Heat oven to 220C/200C fan/gas 7. Put onions in a steamer and cook for 20 minutes, or until tender.
2 Meanwhile, put the garlic and olive oil in a shallow flameproof casserole dish or large frying pan. Gently cook over a medium heat for 1 minute, taking care not to let it colour. Tip in the tomatoes, sugar and half a can of water. Simmer for 10 minutes, then season. Nestle the onion halves, cut-side down, in the sauce and simmer for 5 minutes more.
3 Transfer to a baking dish, if you need to, sprinkle over the breadcrumbs and goat's cheese, then bake for 20 minutes, until bubbling and golden.

PER SERVING 346 kcals, protein 14g, carbs 39g, fat 15g, sat fat 6g, fibre 5g, sugar 19g, salt 1.1g

Cheesy eggy bread with chunky salad

For kids, swap the chunky salad for baked beans or spaghetti shapes in tomato sauce.

TAKES 20 MINUTES • SERVES 1

2 eggs, beaten
50g/2oz vegetarian Cheddar, very finely
    grated
2 chunky slices bread from a small
    crusty loaf or 3 from a baguette

FOR THE SALAD

handful cherry tomatoes, halved
½ avocado, diced
chunk of cucumber, diced
small handful rocket leaves

1 Whisk the eggs and cheese with some seasoning in a shallow dish. Lay the bread in the mix so it soaks up a little egg, and scoop out any extra cheese, pressing it to stick on to the bread. Heat a good non-stick frying pan (if you don't have one, heat a normal pan with a knob of butter and drizzle of oil). Fry the bread for 2–4 minutes on each side until golden.

2 Mix the salad ingredients together with some seasoning and serve alongside.

PER SERVING 675 kcals, protein 36g, carbs 33g, fat 46g, sat fat 17g, fibre 5g, sugar 4g, salt 2.28g

Flatbread pizzas

Some ruffles of air-dried ham would also make a welcome addition to these pretty flatbreads.

TAKES 15 MINUTES • SERVES 5

400g can chickpeas in water, rinsed
    and drained
juice 1 lemon
1 garlic clove, crushed
½ tsp ground cumin
5-pack Middle Eastern flatbreads
75g/2½oz feta, crumbled
handful dill sprigs
200g bag rocket leaves
100g pack pomegranate seeds
1 red onion, thinly sliced
1 tsp olive oil

1 Blitz the chickpeas, half the lemon juice, the garlic, cumin and some seasoning in a food processor or mini chopper, adding a few tablespoons of water to get a spreadable consistency.
2 Warm the flatbreads according to the pack instructions, then spread the chickpea purée over them. Scatter on the feta, dill and half the rocket, pomegranate and onion.
3 Mix together the remaining rocket, pomegranate and onion. Toss through the remaining lemon juice, the olive oil and any juice from the pomegranate seeds. Serve the pizzas with the salad.

PER SERVING 369 kcals, protein 18g, carbs 63g, fat 8g, sat fat 2g, fibre 5g, sugar 8g, salt 1.9g

Quick mushroom & spinach lasagne

You can find fresh lasagne in the chiller cabinet in larger supermarkets, next to the stuffed fresh pastas such as tortellini.

TAKES 45 MINUTES • SERVES 4

1 tbsp olive oil
1 garlic clove, crushed
250g pack mushrooms, sliced
1 tsp thyme leaves, chopped
200g bag spinach leaves
300g tub light soft cheese
4 tbsp grated Parmesan or vegetarian
  alternative
6 fresh lasagne sheets

1 Heat oven to 200C/180C fan/gas 6. Heat the oil in a large frying pan, add the garlic and cook for 1 minute. Add the mushrooms and thyme, then cook for 3 minutes until they start to soften. Throw in the spinach and stir until the heat of the pan wilts the leaves. Remove from the heat and stir in the soft cheese, 1 tablespoon of the Parmesan or vegetarian alternative and some seasoning.
2 Put a quarter of the spinach mix on the bottom of a medium-sized baking dish, lay two pasta sheets on top, then repeat until you have used all the pasta. Finish with the final quarter of the spinach mix, sprinkle over the rest of the Parmesan or vegetarian alternative, then bake for 35 minutes until golden and the pasta is tender.

PER SERVING 301 kcals, protein 16g, carbs 25g, fat 16g, sat fat 8g, fibre 3g, sugar 4g, salt 1.15g

Vegetable ragu

This veggie version of Bolognese sauce can be served with pasta and some Parmesan sprinkled over, or rice. It also freezes really well.

TAKES 50 MINUTES • SERVES 5

1 onion, finely chopped

2 celery sticks, finely chopped

2 carrots, diced

4 garlic cloves, crushed

1 tbsp each tomato purée and balsamic
  vinegar

250g/9oz diced vegetables, such as
  courgettes, peppers and mushrooms

50g/2oz red split lentils

2 × 400g cans chopped tomatoes
  with basil

1 Tip the onion, celery and carrots into a large non-stick pan and add 2–3 tablespoons water, or stock if you have some. Cook gently, stirring often, until the vegetables are soft.

2 Add the garlic, tomato purée and balsamic vinegar, and cook on a high heat for 1 minute more. Add the diced vegetables, lentils and tomatoes, then bring up to the boil.

3 Turn to a simmer, then cook for about 20 minutes. Season the ragu and serve while hot.

PER SERVING 321 kcals, protein 15g, carbs 55g, fat 3g, sat fat 2g, fibre 5g, sugar 12g, salt 0.3g

Italian stuffed courgettes

Remember the courgettes will shrink as they cook – so try to use larger ones for this recipe.

TAKES 45 MINUTES • SERVES 4

4 courgettes, halved lengthways
1 tbsp extra virgin olive oil
mixed salad leaves, to serve

FOR THE STUFFING

50g/2oz dried white breadcrumbs
50g/2oz pine nuts
6 spring onions, trimmed and finely sliced
1 garlic clove, crushed
6 sun-dried tomatoes in oil, drained
1 tbsp thyme leaves
25g/1oz Parmesan, finely grated

1 Heat oven to 220C/200C fan/gas 7. Put the courgettes in a single layer in a shallow ovenproof dish, fairly tightly together, cut-side up. Brush lightly with 1 teaspoon of the oil and bake for 20 minutes.

2 To make the stuffing, mix all the ingredients together in a bowl and season with lots of black pepper.

3 Sprinkle the stuffing on top of the courgettes and drizzle with the remaining olive oil. Bake for a further 10–15 minutes or until the courgettes are softened and the topping is golden and crisp.

PER SERVING 244 kcals, protein 10g, carbs 14g, fat 17g, sat fat 3g, fibre 3g, sugar 5g, salt 0.5g

Mushroom stroganoff

You can add soaked dried mushrooms to this for lots of extra flavour – you can also add the soaking liquid to the stock.

TAKES 30 MINUTES • SERVES 2

2 tsp olive oil

1 onion, finely chopped

2 garlic cloves, crushed

1 tbsp paprika

300g/10oz mixed mushrooms, chopped

150ml/½ pint vegetable stock

1 tbsp Worcestershire sauce or
   vegetarian alternative

3 tbsp half-fat soured cream

small bunch parsley, roughly chopped

250g pouch cooked wild rice

1 Heat the oil in a large non-stick frying pan and soften the onion for about 5 minutes. Add the garlic and paprika, then cook for 1 minute more. Add the mushrooms and cook on a high heat, stirring often, for about 5 minutes.

2 Pour in the stock and Worcestershire sauce or vegetarian alternative. Bring to the boil, bubble for 5 minutes until the sauce thickens, then turn off the heat and stir through the soured cream and most of the parsley. Make sure the pan is not on the heat or the sauce may split.

3 Heat the rice according to the pack instructions, then stir through the remaining parsley and serve the rice with the stroganoff.

PER SERVING 329 kcals, protein 11g, carbs 50g, fat 9g, sat fat 1g, fibre 4g, sugar 8g, salt 0.7g

Feta & semi-dried tomato omelette

When you're home alone and cooking for one, nothing beats an omelette for speed, ease and flavour.

TAKES 10 MINUTES • SERVES 1

1 tsp olive oil
2 eggs, lightly beaten
4 semi-dried tomatoes, roughly
    chopped
25g/1oz feta, crumbled
mixed salad leaves, to serve

1 Heat the oil in a small non-stick frying pan, add the eggs and cook, swirling the eggs with a fork as they set. When the eggs are still slightly runny in the middle, scatter over the tomatoes and feta, then fold the omelette in half. Cook for 1 minute more before sliding on to a plate.

2 Serve with a mixed leaf salad.

PER SERVING 266 kcals, protein 18g, carbs 5g, fat 20g, sat fat 7g, fibre 1g, sugar 4g, salt 1.8g

Chilli pepper pumpkin with Asian veg

For a really healthy supper, what could be better than a gorgeous selection of highly seasoned vegetables?

TAKES 40 MINUTES • SERVES 2

1 small pumpkin or ½ butternut squash, cut into chunks (seeds removed), no need to peel

2 tsp sunflower or vegetable oil

1 tsp each mild chilli powder and Chinese five spice

175g/6oz thin-stemmed broccoli

175g/6oz pak choy, quartered

2 tbsp low-sodium soy sauce

2 tbsp rice wine vinegar

1 tbsp clear honey

1 lime, ½ juice, ½ cut into wedges

few coriander leaves to garnish

1 Heat oven to 220C/200C fan/gas 7. Toss the pumpkin or squash in the oil, then sprinkle on the chilli powder, five spice, 1 teaspoon black pepper and a pinch of salt, and mix well. Tip into a roasting tin in a single layer and cook for 25–30 minutes until tender and starting to caramelise around the edges.

2 About 5 minutes before the pumpkin or squash is cooked, heat a wok or large frying pan and add the broccoli plus 1–2 tablespoons water. Cook for 2–3 minutes, then add the pak choy, soy, vinegar and honey, and cook for a further 2–3 minutes until the veg is tender. Add the lime juice, then divide between two plates with the pumpkin or squash, coriander leaves and lime wedges.

PER SERVING 248 kcals, protein 9g, carbs 42g, fat 5g, sat fat 1g, fibre 7g, sugar 30g, salt 1.9g

Turkish one-pan eggs & peppers

Served with garlic yogurt and some bread, this is a brilliant light dish for lunch or supper.

TAKES 25 MINUTES • SERVES 4

2 tbsp olive oil

2 onions, sliced

1 red or green pepper, halved, deseeded and sliced

1–2 red chillies, deseeded and sliced

400g can chopped tomatoes

1–2 tsp caster sugar

4 eggs

6 tbsp thick creamy yogurt

2 garlic cloves, crushed

small bunch parsley, roughly chopped

1 Heat the oil in a heavy-based frying pan. Stir in the onions, pepper and chillies. Cook until they begin to soften. Add the tomatoes and sugar, mixing well. Cook until the liquid has reduced, then season.

2 Using a wooden spoon, create four pockets in the tomato mixture and crack the eggs into them. Cover the pan and cook the eggs over a low heat until just set.

3 In a small bowl beat the yogurt with the garlic and season. Sprinkle the eggs with parsley and serve from the frying pan with a dollop of the garlic-flavoured yogurt.

PER SERVING 222 kcals, protein 12g, carbs 12g, fat 15g, sat fat 4g, fibre 3g, sugar 9g, salt 0.39g

Butternut squash & spinach filo pie

Filo makes a light and crispy topping to this tasty pie but you could also use puff pastry for the lid – if so, add an extra 10 minutes to the cooking time.

TAKES 1 HOUR • SERVES 4

1 butternut squash (about 1kg/2lb 4oz), peeled, deseeded and cut into 2cm/¾in dice
2 red onions, cut into wedges
1 tsp chilli flakes
400g bag spinach leaves
100g/4oz feta, crumbled
4 sheets filo pastry
1 tbsp olive oil
green salad, to serve (optional)

1 Heat oven to 220C/200C fan/gas 7. Put the squash, onions and chilli flakes in an ovenproof pie dish (or four individual dishes). Season and cook for 20 minutes until the squash is tender and the onions are starting to brown at the edges.

2 Meanwhile, put the spinach in a colander and pour over a kettleful of boiling water. Squeeze out any excess liquid and stir into the squash mix. Dot over the feta, crumple up the pastry and put on top, then brush with the oil. Return to the oven and cook for a further 15 minutes until the pastry is golden and crisp. Serve with a green salad, if you like.

PER SERVING 294 kcals, protein 12g, carbs 40g, fat 10g, sat fat 4g, fibre 8g, sugar 17g, salt 1.4g

Leek, goat's cheese, walnut & lemon tart

A simple salad of chicory and sliced pear would go really well with this easy tart.

TAKES 50 MINUTES ● SERVES 4

1 tbsp olive oil, plus extra for drizzling
25g/1oz butter
2 medium leeks, sliced
2 tbsp chopped thyme leaves
zest 2 lemons and juice 1 lemon
375g pack ready-rolled puff pastry
200g/7oz soft spreadable goat's
 cheese
50g/2oz walnut pieces
chopped parsley, to garnish

1 Heat oven to 220C/200C fan/gas 7. Heat the olive oil in a large frying pan, then add the butter and leeks, and cook over a medium heat until softened but not coloured. Stir in the thyme and half the lemon zest, then increase the heat. Add the lemon juice and cook for about 30 seconds until the lemon juice reduces, then season well. Remove from the heat and cool slightly.

2 Unroll the pastry and lay on a baking sheet. Lightly mark a 1cm/½in border around the edges with the tip of a sharp knife, then prick the base all over with a fork.

3 Spread the leeks on top of the pastry, within the border. Crumble over the cheese, scatter with the walnuts, then season with pepper, drizzle with some olive oil, brushing the edges with a little oil as well. Put the tart in the oven for 15–20 minutes until the pastry puffs up around the edges and is golden brown. Scatter with parsley and the remaining lemon zest and serve hot, warm or cool.

PER SERVING 683 kcals, protein 19g, carbs 35g, fat 52g, sat fat 24g, fibre 2g, sugar 3g, salt 1.6g

Fruit & nut butternut squash quinoa

Cooking with quinoa makes a superhealthy change from rice or couscous.

TAKES 40 MINUTES • SERVES 4

- 1 butternut squash, peeled and cut into small cubes
- 2 onions, cut into thin wedges
- 2 tbsp olive oil, plus a little extra for drizzling
- 200g/7oz quinoa
- 4 tbsp natural yogurt
- 1 tbsp tahini paste
- juice 1 lemon
- 85g/3oz toasted flaked almonds
- 85g/3oz shelled pistachio nuts
- 10 dried apricots, sliced
- handful mint leaves, roughly chopped

1 Heat oven to 220C/200C fan/gas 7. Tip the squash and onions into a large shallow roasting dish with the oil. Season and roast for around 30 minutes, or until tender, shaking the dish once or twice.

2 Cook the quinoa according to the pack instructions. When cooked, run under cold water and thoroughly drain.

3 Stir together the yogurt, tahini and most of the lemon juice, and seasoning in a small bowl and set aside. Mix the quinoa, nuts, apricots, mint and some seasoning in a large bowl. Squeeze over the remaining lemon juice, drizzle with a little oil and stir in. Scatter over the squash–onion mix and serve the yogurt sauce on the side.

PER SERVING 662 kcals, protein 23g, carbs 62g, fat 35g, sat fat 5g, fibre 10g, sugar 29g, salt 0.2g

Pumpkin, halloumi & chilli frittata

With everything cooked in one pan, this tasty supper leaves you with very little washing up.

TAKES 40 MINUTES • SERVES 4

2 tbsp olive or rapeseed oil
175g/6oz halloumi, sliced
500g/1lb 2oz pumpkin or butternut
    squash, diced
2 red chillies, deseeded and finely
    chopped
1 garlic clove, finely chopped
2 tsp balsamic or cider vinegar
small bunch mint, roughly chopped
6 eggs, beaten

1 Heat half the oil in a large frying pan. Cook the halloumi for 1–2 minutes on each side until golden, remove from the pan and set aside.

2 Add the remaining oil to the pan, then cook the pumpkin or squash for about 10 minutes, until soft and starting to colour. Add the chillies and garlic, and cook for a further 2 minutes. Pour over the vinegar, then tip the halloumi back into the pan, scatter over the mint and pour on the eggs. Cook for 5 minutes until the base is set.

3 Heat the grill to high. Flash the frittata under the grill for 5 minutes until puffed up and golden. Serve immediately or allow to cool and serve cold with a salad, if you like.

PER SERVING 339 kcals, protein 21g, carbs 3g, fat 27g, sat fat 10g, fibre 1g, sugar 3g, salt 1.92g

Very simple Margherita pizza

This classic pizza is just fine as is, or scatter over a few of your favourite toppings as well.

TAKES 35 MINUTES • SERVES 2

olive oil, for greasing

200g/7oz plain flour

7g packet easy-blend dried yeast

1 tsp caster sugar

125ml/4fl oz warm water

85ml/3fl oz passata

small bunch basil, half torn,
  half left whole

100g/4oz mozzarella, half grated,
  half chopped

2 tbsp grated Parmesan or vegetarian
  alternative

side salad, to serve

1 Heat oven to 240C/220C fan/gas 9. Oil a 20 × 24cm baking tin. Mix the flour, yeast, ¼ teaspoon salt and the sugar in a bowl, then stir in the water. Bring the mixture together, knead until smooth, then press into the oiled tin.

2 Spread passata over the dough, leaving a thin border round the edge. Season the passata, then sprinkle with the torn basil, the mozzarella and the Parmesan or vegetarian alternative, and bake for 15–20 minutes or until cooked through. Scatter with the remaining basil leaves and serve with a side salad.

PER SERVING 577 kcals, protein 26g, carbs 77g, fat 18g, sat fat 10g, fibre 4g, sugar 6g, salt 1.8g

Spiced carrot, chickpea & almond pilaf

Pilafs are light but still comforting and are also cleverly made in just one pan.

TAKES 35 MINUTES • SERVES 4

1 tbsp olive oil

2 onions, finely chopped

3 carrots (about 300g/10oz), coarsely grated

2 tbsp harissa paste

300g/10oz basmati rice, rinsed

700ml/1¼ pint vegetable stock

400g can chickpeas, rinsed and drained

25g/1oz toasted flaked almonds

200g pot thick Greek yogurt

1 Heat the oil in a lidded casserole dish. Add the onions and cook for 8 minutes, until soft. Tip in the carrots, harissa and rice, and stir for a couple of minutes. Pour over the stock, bring to the boil, then cover with the lid and simmer over the lowest heat for 10 minutes.

2 Fork through the chickpeas and cook gently for 3–5 minutes more, until the grains of rice are tender and all the liquid has been absorbed. Season, turn off the heat, cover and leave to sit for a few minutes.

3 Sprinkle the almonds over the rice mixture and serve with a dollop of yogurt.

PER SERVING 543 kcals, protein 15g, carbs 83g, fat 13g, sat fat 4g, fibre 7g, sugar 14g, salt 1.2g

Mushroom, spinach & potato pie

This crispy pastry-topped pie is a veggie option that will suit everyone, and it's also low fat.

TAKES 50 MINUTES • SERVES 4

400g/14oz baby leaf spinach
1 tbsp olive oil
500g/1lb 2oz mushrooms, such as chestnut, shiitake and button
2 garlic cloves, crushed
250ml/9fl oz vegetable stock
1 tbsp grain mustard
1 tsp freshly grated nutmeg
300g/10oz cooked new potatoes, cut into bite-sized pieces
2 heaped tbsp light crème fraîche
3 sheets filo pastry
300g/10oz each green beans and broccoli, steamed

1 Heat oven to 200C/180C fan/gas 6. Wilt the spinach in a colander by pouring over a kettleful of boiling water. Allow to drain.
2 Heat half the oil in a large non-stick pan and fry the mushrooms on a high heat until golden. Add the garlic and cook for 1 minute, then tip in the stock, mustard, nutmeg and potatoes. Bubble for a few minutes until reduced. Season, then remove from the heat and add the crème fraîche and spinach. Tip into a pie dish and allow to cool for a few minutes.
3 Brush the filo with the remaining oil, quarter the sheets then loosely scrunch up and lay on top of the pie filling. Bake for 20–25 minutes until golden. Serve with the steamed vegetables.

PER SERVING 215 kcals, protein 9g, carbs 29g, fat 8g, sat fat 2g, fibre 5g, sugar 4g, salt 0.77g

Spiced Indian potato wraps

This casual supper is filling and cheap, and you don't need any cutlery to eat it.

TAKES 50 MINUTES • SERVES 3

4 sweet potatoes, cut into chunky
  wedges
1 red chilli, finely chopped
2 tbsp olive oil
2 tsp cumin seeds
1 tbsp garam masala
1 red onion, thinly sliced
juice 1 lime
2 tsp sugar
6–9 chapatis
150g/5oz natural yogurt
large bunch coriander

1 Heat oven to 200C/180C fan/gas 6. Toss the sweet potatoes in a roasting tin with the chilli, 1 teaspoon of the oil, the cumin seeds, garam masala and plenty of seasoning. Roast for 25–35 minutes, turning the wedges halfway through, until tender and golden.

2 Meanwhile, fry the onion in the remaining oil for a few minutes until partly softened, stir in the lime juice and sugar with some seasoning, then turn off the heat.

3 Warm the chapatis according to the pack instructions, then assemble the wraps by adding a couple of wedges of sweet potato in each, followed by a scattering of onions, a dollop of yogurt and a small handful of coriander leaves. Roll up and eat.

PER SERVING 445 kcals, protein 13g, carbs 68g, fat 15g, sat fat 3g, fibre 4g, sugar 20g, salt 0.81g

Risotto primavera

Use this risotto as a blueprint and add whatever spring veg you want. Broad beans and asparagus tips would both work well.

TAKES 35 MINUTES • **SERVES 4**

1 litre/1¾ pints vegetable stock
4 tbsp olive oil
1 onion, chopped
2 carrots, diced
2 medium courgettes, diced
300g/10oz risotto rice
bunch spring onions, thinly sliced
100g/4oz frozen peas
4 tbsp grated Parmesan or vegetarian
   alternative, to garnish

1 Bring the stock to the boil, then turn down to a low simmer. Heat the oil in a medium pan. Add the onion, carrots and courgettes, season and fry for 3 minutes. Add the rice and cook, stirring constantly, for a further 2 minutes, then add a ladleful of stock. Stir until absorbed and continue until you have nearly used up all of the stock and the rice is just cooked with a slight bite to it.
2 Add the spring onions and peas and cook for a few minutes more then spoon into bowls and serve with the cheese sprinkled over.

PER SERVING 475 kcals, protein 20g, carbs 62g, fat 16g, sat fat 7g, fibre 6g, sugar 10g, salt 1.6g

Springtime spaghetti & meatballs

For a healthier version, substitute the minced pork with turkey – it's a great source of protein and very low in fat.

TAKES 35 MINUTES • SERVES 4

400g/14oz minced pork
1 small onion, grated
4 garlic cloves, crushed
zest ½ lemon
50g/2oz grated Parmesan
1 tbsp olive oil
400g/14oz spaghetti
150ml/¼ pint double cream
200g/7oz fresh or frozen peas,
    defrosted if frozen
handful parsley, roughly chopped

1 Mix the mince, onion, garlic and zest with half the Parmesan and some seasoning, then shape into 16 walnut-sized meatballs. Heat the oil in a non-stick pan and fry the meatballs for 10–12 minutes until golden.

2 Meanwhile, cook the pasta according to the pack instructions, drain and reserve 150ml/¼ pint of the cooking liquid. Add the cream and 100ml/3½fl oz of the pasta water to the meatballs, scraping the bottom of the pan to get all the sticky bits off. Bubble until thick and the meatballs are cooked through.

3 Add the peas, cook for a further 2 minutes, then add the parsley. Stir through the pasta with a splash more pasta water to make the whole thing saucy. Sprinkle over the remaining Parmesan and serve.

PER SERVING 699 kcals, protein 36g, carbs 52g, fat 38g, sat fat 19g, fibre 6g, sugar 4g, salt 0.4g

Tuna pasta bake

Few dishes are more family friendly than this comforting bake made from mostly storecupboard ingredients – leave the mustard out for the very little ones.

TAKES 30 MINUTES • SERVES 4

400g/14oz fusilli pasta
100g/4oz frozen peas
50g/2oz butter
50g/2oz plain flour
600ml/1 pint milk
1 tsp Dijon mustard
2 × 195g cans tuna, drained
4 spring onions, sliced
198g can sweetcorn, drained
100g/4oz Cheddar, grated

1 Bring a pan of water to the boil. Add the pasta and cook, according to the pack instructions, until tender. Add the peas for the final 3 minutes of cooking time.

2 Meanwhile, melt the butter in a pan over a medium heat. Stir in the flour and cook for 2 minutes. Add the milk, whisking constantly, then slowly bring to the boil, stirring often, until the sauce thickens. Remove from the heat, add the mustard and season well.

3 Heat the grill to medium. Drain the pasta and peas, then return to the pan and stir in the tuna, spring onions, sweetcorn and sauce. Tip into four individual dishes or one large shallow baking dish, top with the Cheddar and cook under the grill for 5 minutes or until golden and bubbling.

PER SERVING 655 kcals, protein 41g, carbs 55g, fat 30g, sat fat 15g, fibre 4g, sugar 11g, salt 1.7g

Chorizo & broad bean risotto

A simple yet very indulgent dish, with the spicy flavours of chorizo sausages.

TAKES 40 MINUTES • SERVES 4

1 tbsp olive oil
100g/4oz smoked bacon, diced
2 shallots, chopped
2 garlic cloves, crushed
350g/12oz small cooking chorizo
300g/10oz risotto rice
1 litre/1¾ pints hot chicken stock
300g/10oz frozen broad beans

1 Heat the oil in a medium-sized pan, then add the bacon, shallots, garlic and chorizo. Gently cook for 8 minutes, stirring occasionally so everything cooks evenly.

2 Stir in the rice, coating it all over with the juices in the pan. Add just enough stock to cover the rice, bring to a simmer and gently cook, stirring, until all the liquid is absorbed. Continue adding the stock a ladleful at a time and stirring. Just before the final ladleful of stock, add the broad beans and stir through, cooking for 3–4 minutes until tender. Remove the chorizo, slice thinly, return to the pan and mix through before serving.

PER SERVING 830 kcals, protein 41g, carbs 71g, fat 45g, sat fat 17g, fibre 8g, sugar 4g, salt 5.06g

Sushi rice bowl with beef, egg & chilli sauce

Unlike basmati or long grain rice, the virtue of sushi rice is its stickiness – as well as its unique flavour.

TAKES 25 MINUTES • SERVES 2

140g/5oz sushi rice
250g/9oz rump steak, thinly sliced
1 garlic clove, chopped
1 tbsp soy sauce
good pinch caster sugar
2 tbsp sesame oil
2 eggs
1 large carrot, cut into long matchsticks
1 large courgette, cut into long matchsticks
2 tbsp sweet and spicy chilli sauce

1 Boil the sushi rice in a large pan with plenty of water – it should take about 8–10 minutes – until it is cooked but still has a slight bite to it. Drain, tip back in to the pan, cover with a lid and set aside.
2 Mix the steak with the garlic, soy sauce, sugar and a grind of black pepper. You will need two frying pans or one frying pan and a wok: divide the oil between the two pans and heat until just smoking. Fry the eggs to your liking, then set aside and keep warm. In the other pan, brown the beef for 1–2 minutes, then remove and keep warm. Tip the vegetables into the pan, stir-fry for 1 minute, then push to one side, add the rice and cook for 1 minute more to heat through.
3 Divide the rice, veg and beef between two bowls. Slide the eggs on top and drizzle with the chilli sauce. Each person can then toss everything together, so the egg yolk mixes with the hot rice and sauce.

PER SERVING 621 kcals, protein 41g, carbs 63g, fat 23g, sat fat 5g, fibre 2g, sugar 8g, salt 3.2g

Bacon & mushroom risotto

This easy-to-make risotto makes the most of ingredients you've probably already got in your kitchen.

TAKES 40 MINUTES ● **SERVES 4**

1 tbsp olive oil
1 onion, chopped
8 rashers streaky bacon, chopped
250g/9oz chestnut mushrooms, sliced
300g/10oz risotto rice
1 litre/1¾ pints hot chicken stock
grated Parmesan, to garnish

1 Heat the oil in a medium pan and cook the onion and bacon for 5 minutes to soften. Add the mushrooms and cook for a further 5 minutes until they start to release their juices. Stir in the rice and cook until all the juices have been absorbed.
2 Add the stock, a ladleful at a time, stirring well and waiting for most of the stock to be absorbed before adding the next ladleful – it will take about 20 minutes for all the stock to be added. Once the rice is cooked, season and serve with the grated Parmesan.

PER SERVING 452 kcals, protein 21g, carbs 62g, fat 13g, sat fat 4g, fibre 3g, sugar 3g, salt 1.9g

Lemony prawn & chorizo rice pot

Think of this as a much easier version of the classic Spanish rice dish, paella.

TAKES 35 MINUTES ● SERVES 4

1 tbsp olive oil
1 onion, sliced
2 small red peppers, deseeded and
    sliced
50g/2oz chorizo, thinly sliced
2 garlic cloves, crushed
1 red chilli, chopped (deseeded if you
    don't like it too hot)
½ tsp ground turmeric
250g/9oz long grain rice
200g/7oz raw peeled prawns,
    defrosted if frozen
100g/4oz frozen peas
zest and juice 1 lemon, plus extra
    wedges to garnish

1 Boil the kettle. Heat the oil in a shallow pan with a lid, add the onion, peppers, chorizo, garlic and chilli, then fry over a high heat for 3 minutes. Add the turmeric and rice, stirring to ensure the rice is coated. Pour in 500ml/18fl oz boiling water, cover, then cook for 12 minutes.
2 Uncover, then stir – the rice should be almost tender. Stir in the prawns and peas, with a splash more water if the rice is looking dry, then cook for 1 minute more until the prawns are just pink and the rice tender. Stir in the lemon zest and juice with some seasoning and serve with extra lemon wedges on the side.

PER SERVING 381 kcals, protein 21g, carbs 55g, fat 7g, sat fat 2g, fibre 3g, sugar 6g, salt 2.2g

Thai pork patties with sweet chilli sauce & noodles

If lemongrass is hard to find, the finely grated zest of 1 lemon makes a good substitute.

TAKES 30 MINUTES • SERVES 2

250g/9oz minced pork
1 garlic clove, finely chopped
3 lemongrass stalks, outer layers
   removed, bottom thirds of stalks
   finely chopped
1 tbsp Thai fish sauce
handful coriander, chopped
1 tbsp sesame oil
1 tsp sugar
100g/4oz fine rice noodles
4 spring onions, chopped
sweet chilli dipping sauce, to drizzle

1 Heat the grill. In a bowl, mix together the pork, garlic, lemongrass, fish sauce and half the coriander. Season with pepper. Mix well and form into eight patties. Rub each one with the oil and a sprinkling of sugar, then put on a rack in a baking tin.

2 Grill the patties for 3 minutes on each side until golden brown. Meanwhile, in a large bowl, soak the rice noodles according to the pack instructions. Drain the warm noodles and serve with the patties, spring onions, remaining coriander and a drizzle of sweet chilli dipping sauce.

PER SERVING 446 kcals, protein 28g, carbs 46g, fat 18g, sat fat 5g, fibre 1g, sugar 3g, salt 1.72g

Chicken, edamame & ginger pilaf

Edamame or soya beans can be found near the frozen peas and sweetcorn in the freezer aisle of larger supermarkets.

TAKES 25 MINUTES • SERVES 4

2 tbsp vegetable oil
1 onion, thinly sliced
thumb-sized piece ginger, grated
1 red chilli, deseeded and finely sliced
3 skinless chicken breasts, cut into
    bite-sized pieces
250g/9oz basmati rice
600ml/1 pint vegetable stock
100g/4oz frozen edamame/soya beans
coriander leaves to sprinkle
fat-free Greek yogurt, to serve
    (optional)

1 Heat the oil in a medium pan, then add the onion, ginger and chilli, along with some seasoning. Cook for 5 minutes, then add the chicken and rice.
2 Cook for 2 minutes more, then add the stock and bring to the boil. Turn the heat to low, cover and cook for 8–10 minutes until the rice is just cooked. During the final 3 minutes of cooking, add the edamame beans. Sprinkle some coriander leaves on top and serve with a dollop of Greek yogurt, if you like.

PER SERVING 436 kcals, protein 32g, carbs 52g, fat 9g, sat fat 1g, fibre 3g, sugar 4g, salt 0.5g

Cheesy leek & bacon pasta

A quick family pasta supper made using just five ingredients.

TAKES 30 MINUTES ● SERVES 4

1 tbsp olive oil

300g/10oz leeks, halved and finely
  sliced

8 rashers smoked streaky bacon, sliced

400g/14oz pasta shapes (we used
  penne)

100g/4oz herb & garlic soft cheese

1 Heat the oil in a large non-stick frying pan. Add the leeks and 2 tablespoons water, and cook for about 10 minutes until very soft. Add the bacon, turn up the heat and fry until cooked.

2 Meanwhile, cook the pasta according to the pack instructions. Drain and reserve a mug of the cooking water.

3 Spoon the cheese into the leek and bacon mix, adding some of the reserved cooking water. Season and stir gently over a low heat until melted. Toss through the cooked pasta, adding a little more cooking water before serving, if needed, to help the sauce coat the pasta.

PER SERVING 556 kcals, protein 23g, carbs 76g, fat 18g, sat fat 7g, fibre 4g, sugar 4g, salt 1.5g

Teriyaki prawns & broccoli noodles

For an even quicker supper you could use shop-bought teriyaki sauce rather than simmering the first four ingredients together.

TAKES 20 MINUTES • SERVES 2

50ml/2fl oz low-sodium soy sauce
50ml/2fl oz mirin
2 tbsp lemon juice
1½ tbsp caster sugar
200g/7oz soba noodles
140g/5oz thin-stemmed broccoli
140g/50z cooked king prawns
1 small red chilli, thinly sliced, to serve

1 In a small pan, heat the soy sauce, mirin, lemon juice and sugar. Simmer for 5 minutes until syrupy, then remove from the heat and keep warm.

2 Bring a large pan of salted water to the boil, then cook the noodles and broccoli for about 3 minutes, adding the prawns a few seconds before draining. Divide the mixture between two plates, pour the warm teriyaki sauce over the top, sprinkle with the red chilli and serve.

PER SERVING 586 kcals, protein 31g, carbs 103g, fat 3g, sat fat none, fibre 4g, sugar 27g, salt 8g

Turkey chilli & rice tacos

Chipotle paste is a smoky chilli paste that can be found alongside other Mexican ingredients in the world food aisle.

TAKES 40 MINUTES • SERVES 4

2 tbsp chipotle paste
400g/14oz minced turkey
100g/4oz long grain rice, rinsed
420g can kidney beans in water, rinsed and drained
600ml/1 pint chicken stock
140g/5oz frozen sweetcorn, defrosted
small bunch coriander, chopped
8 taco shells
½ iceberg lettuce, shredded
150ml pot soured cream
grated cheese and guacamole, to serve

1 Heat the paste in a frying pan with a lid. When hot, add the mince and cook until browned, breaking it up well as it cooks. Stir in the rice and beans, and mix well, then add the stock.
2 Cover and simmer for 20–25 minutes until the rice is tender, then stir in the sweetcorn and scatter over the coriander. Heat the taco shells according to the pack instructions, then serve with the mince mixture, shredded lettuce and soured cream. Let everyone build their own dinner, adding grated cheese and guacamole.

PER SERVING 503 kcals, protein 38g, carbs 56g, fat 16g, sat fat 5g, fibre 7g, sugar 7g, salt 1.16g

Roasted tomato & Cheddar rice with garden salad

Here risotto has been given a British spin in a dish that's bound to be a sure-fire hit with kids.

TAKES 30 MINUTES • SERVES 4

400g/14oz cherry tomatoes
2 onions, chopped
1 tbsp oregano leaves (or 1½ tsp dried), plus a little extra to garnish
1 tbsp olive oil
250g/9oz easy-cook long grain rice
1 litre/1¾ pints hot vegetable stock
2 avocados, sliced
about 3 small bunches mixed soft herbs
1 baby cos lettuce, shredded
juice 1 lemon
200g/7oz mature Cheddar, grated

1 Heat oven to 200C/180C fan/gas 6. Spread the tomatoes on a baking sheet and roast for 15 minutes, then remove. Heat grill to high.

2 Meanwhile, soften the onions and oregano in the oil, stir in the rice and stock, and boil for 15 minutes, stirring occasionally, until the rice is cooked.

3 Mix together the avocados, herbs, shredded lettuce and lemon juice for the salad.

4 Stir most of the cheese and roasted tomatoes into the rice, tip into an ovenproof dish, scatter the remaining cheese and tomatoes on top with some more oregano and flash under the grill to brown. Spoon on to plates with the garden salad served on the side.

PER SERVING 681 kcals, protein 28g, carbs 64g, fat 37g, sat fat 14g, fibre 5g, sugar 8g, salt 1.61g

Five spice beef & sugar snap noodles

A new quick, flavour-packed recipe for mince. This dish would also work with minced pork or turkey.

TAKES 25 MINUTES • SERVES 4

250g/9oz lean minced beef

3 nests medium egg noodles

thumb-sized piece ginger, finely grated

3 garlic cloves, finely grated

1 heaped tsp Chinese five spice powder

¼ tsp chilli powder

225g pack sugar snap peas or mangetout

400ml/14fl oz beef stock

3 tbsp light soy sauce

sesame oil, to sprinkle

1 red chilli, deseeded and shredded, to garnish (optional)

1 Heat a large non-stick frying pan or wok. Add the mince and fry for 10 minutes until very well browned. Don't add any oil.

2 Meanwhile, cook the noodles according to the pack instructions. Drain.

3 Add the ginger, garlic, five spice, chilli powder and sugar snaps or mangetout, then fry for a few minutes more until fragrant and the pods are bright green. Splash in the stock, then add the noodles and soy sauce. Pile into bowls, sprinkling with the sesame oil and red chilli, if you like.

PER SERVING 458 kcals, protein 30g, carbs 71g, fat 8g, sat fat 8g, fibre 4g, sugar 5g, salt 4.08g

Thai prawn fried rice

Healthier and cheaper than a takeaway, this is also quicker to make than the time it takes for a home delivery.

TAKES 20 MINUTES ● SERVES 4

2 tsp vegetable oil
2 eggs, beaten
1–2 tbsp Thai red curry paste
800g/1lb 12oz cooked rice
300g/10oz cooked prawns, defrosted if frozen
175g/6oz frozen sliced green beans, defrosted
juice 1 lime, plus extra wedges to garnish
1 tbsp Thai fish sauce, plus extra to taste
shredded cucumber, sliced red chilli and coriander leaves, to garnish (optional)

1 Heat the oil in a large wok or frying pan over a medium heat. Pour in the eggs, tilt the pan so it forms a thin omelette and cook for about 1 minute until set. Tip out on to a chopping board, roll up, then slice into ribbons. Set aside.

2 Heat the curry paste with 1 tablespoon water until hot, then tip in the rice, stir to break up and toss to coat.

3 Add the prawns and beans, and heat through. Add the lime juice and fish sauce, then stir though the egg strips. Serve the fried rice in bowls with extra lime wedges as a garnish and fish sauce to taste. Scatter with some shredded cucumber, sliced chilli and coriander leaves, if you like.

PER SERVING 401 kcals, protein 27g, carbs 61g, fat 7g, sat fat 2g, fibre 1g, sugar 1g, salt 2.39g

Lemon spaghetti with tuna & broccoli

To make this dish extra special try to find tuna canned in olive oil or, if you are being healthy, use tuna in spring water.

TAKES 15 MINUTES • SERVES 4

350g/12oz spaghetti
250g/9oz broccoli, cut into small florets
2 shallots, finely chopped
85g/3oz pitted green olives, halved
2 tbsp capers, drained
198g can tuna
zest and juice 1 lemon
1 tbsp olive oil, plus extra for drizzling

1 Boil the spaghetti in salted water for 6 minutes. Add the broccoli and boil for 4 minutes more or until both are just tender.

2 Meanwhile, mix the shallots, olives, capers, tuna and lemon zest and juice in a roomy serving bowl. Drain the pasta and broccoli, add to the bowl and toss really well with the olive oil and lots of black pepper. Serve with a little extra olive oil drizzled over.

PER SERVING 440 kcals, protein 23g, carbs 62g, fat 11g, sat fat 2g, fibre 5g, sugar 4g, salt 1.4g

Creamy pasta with asparagus & peas

Make the most of seasonal British asparagus with this simple five-ingredient seasonal supper.

TAKES 20 MINUTES • SERVES 2

250g/9oz fusilli or your favourite pasta
   shape
300g/10oz asparagus spears, woody
   ends removed, cut into lengths
175g/6oz frozen peas
zest and juice ½ lemon
100g/4oz soft cheese with chives

1 Cook the pasta according to the pack instructions. About 2 minutes before the end of the cooking time, add the asparagus and peas. Boil everything together for the final 2 minutes, then scoop out and reserve a cup of the cooking liquid from the pan before draining the pasta and veg.

2 Return the pasta and veg to the pan and add the lemon zest, soft cheese and some seasoning. Add a squeeze of lemon juice to taste and stir in 2–3 tablespoons of the reserved cooking liquid to loosen the sauce before serving.

PER SERVING 658 kcals, protein 25g, carbs 75g, fat 28g, sat fat 15g, fibre 7g, sugar 7g, salt 0.5g

Turkey Singapore noodles

Turkey curry is a traditional British dish, but putting turkey through curried noodles brings it bang up to date.

TAKES 35 MINUTES ● **SERVES 4**

200g/7oz rice noodles

2 tsp sesame oil

2 eggs, beaten

1 tbsp vegetable oil

thumb-sized piece ginger, minced

1 red chilli, chopped, plus extra, sliced, to garnish

200g bag stir-fry vegetables (look for one with bean sprouts)

6 spring onions, finely sliced

140g/5oz cooked turkey meat, shredded

50g/9oz cooked ham, diced

3 tbsp Madras curry powder or paste

2 tbsp soy sauce, plus extra to serve

coriander sprigs to scatter

1 Soak the noodles in boiling water until tender, then drain and toss in 1 teaspoon of the sesame oil. Set aside. Beat the eggs with the rest of the sesame oil and some seasoning. Heat half the vegetable oil in a wok and pour in the eggs to make a flat omelette. Cook on one side, then flip over, cook all the way through and transfer to a plate.

2 Put the wok back on the heat with the rest of the vegetable oil and quickly fry the ginger and chopped chilli. Add all the vegetables to the wok, fry for 1 minute more, then add the turkey and ham. Tip the noodles into the pan and stir through the curry powder or paste and soy. Cook everything together for 1–2 minutes, then shred the omelette and stir it through the noodles. Serve the noodles scattered with coriander sprigs, sliced chilli and some extra soy sauce to taste.

PER SERVING 476 kcals, protein 36g, carbs 50g, fat 13g, sat fat 3g, fibre 4g, sugar 8g, salt 3g

Potato, pepper & chorizo stew with fried eggs

Omit the eggs and this chorizo stew is also great cooked with roast chicken pieces.

TAKES 50 MINUTES • **SERVES 4**

2 tbsp olive oil

1 large onion, sliced

3 peppers (we used a mixed pack of yellow, green and red), deseeded and cut into chunks

4 garlic cloves, thinly sliced

225g/8oz cooking chorizo, cubed

650g/1lb 7oz potatoes, cut into chunks

600ml/1 pint chicken stock

4 eggs

handful flat-leaf parsley, roughly chopped, to sprinkle

1 Heat half the oil in a pan with a lid and add the onion and peppers. Fry for 10–15 minutes until soft, then add the garlic and chorizo, and sizzle until the chorizo releases its oils.

2 Add the potatoes and stir for 1 minute. Pour over the stock, cover with a lid and simmer for 15 minutes, or until the potatoes are tender. Remove the lid and season. Bring to the boil and cook rapidly until most of the liquid has evaporated.

3 Meanwhile, fry the eggs in the remaining oil. Spoon the stew into bowls, then put a fried egg on top of each and serve sprinkled with parsley.

PER SERVING 493 kcals, protein 26g, carbs 38g, fat 25g, sat fat 8g, fibre 6g, sugar 11g, salt 1.4g

Sticky orange chicken & root veg traybake

If you come across golden or stripy beetroot use those, as they look very pretty in this one-pan roast.

TAKES 45 MINUTES ● SERVES 3

3 medium carrots, cut into batons
3 small beetroots, scrubbed and
    thickly sliced
1 tbsp olive oil
1 tsp cumin seeds
2 tbsp orange marmalade
1 tbsp sherry vinegar
3 chicken breasts, pounded slightly
    to flatten a bit
50g/2oz Greek yogurt
handful rocket leaves, chopped
couscous, to serve (optional)

1 Heat oven to 190C/170C fan/gas 5. Arrange the carrots and beetroots on a lipped baking sheet. Drizzle with the oil, add the cumin seeds, season and toss to combine. Roast for 25 minutes until browned around the edges.

2 Put the marmalade and vinegar in a small bowl and mix to combine.

3 Put the chicken in a large bowl and season. Pour over the marmalade sauce and mix to coat well. After the veg has been cooking for 25 minutes, put the chicken pieces on top, baste in the sticky juices and roast for a further 10 minutes.

4 Mix the yogurt with the rocket. Serve the warm chicken and veg with the yogurt and some couscous, if you like.

PER SERVING 340 kcals, protein 34g, carbs 37g, fat 7g, sat fat 3g, fibre 3g, sugar, salt 0.5g

Fennel-crusted pork chops with winter celeriac slaw

This may make a bit more slaw than you need but it keeps well in the fridge for snacking on or serving as part of another meal.

TAKES 50 MINUTES • SERVES 4

1 tbsp olive oil
1 tsp each fennel seeds and dried oregano
pinch chilli flakes
4 pork shoulder chops

FOR THE SLAW

125ml/4fl oz light mayonnaise
1 tbsp white wine vinegar
1 tbsp Worcestershire sauce
1 tbsp wholegrain mustard
pinch sugar
½ small celeriac, cut into matchsticks or shredded
1 large carrot, cut into matchsticks or shredded
1 small red onion, diced

1 Heat oven to 190C/170C fan/gas 5. Put the oil, fennel seeds, oregano, chilli and some seasoning on a shallow plate. Rub each pork chop on both sides in the mixture. Put in a roasting tin and roast for 40 minutes.

2 Meanwhile, make the slaw. Put the mayonnaise, vinegar, Worcestershire sauce, mustard, sugar and a good pinch of salt and pepper in a large bowl. Mix well, then toss in the vegetables.

3 When the pork chops are done, divide the slaw among four plates and add a pork chop to each.

PER SERVING 526 kcals, protein 33g, carbs 8g, fat 40g, sat fat 11g, fibre 6g, sugar 6.5g, salt 1.5g

Crispy pretzel chicken with honey–mustard sauce

Here's a clever, new way to irresistibly crispy-coat pieces of chicken.

TAKES 50 MINUTES • SERVES 4

100g/4oz salted pretzels
8 boneless skinless chicken thighs
flour, for dusting
2 eggs, beaten with a fork
1 tbsp olive oil
100g/4oz wholegrain mustard
4 tbsp clear honey
1 tsp white wine vinegar
green veg or salad and potatoes,
   to serve

1 Heat oven to 200C/180C fan/gas 6. Crush the pretzels in a food processor or bash up in a plastic bag using a rolling pin. Transfer the pretzel crumbs to a plate. Season the chicken, toss in flour, dip into the egg, then roll in the pretzel crumbs. Put on a baking sheet, drizzle over the oil and bake for 35 minutes until crisp and tender.

2 In a small bowl, mix the mustard, honey and vinegar to make a sauce. Serve the chicken with the sauce and some green veg or salad and potatoes.

PER SERVING 454 kcals, protein 43g, carbs 38g, fat 14g, sat fat 3g, fibre 1.7g, sugar 18g, salt 2.6g

Jerk beef burger with pineapple relish & chips

The winning combo of burger and chips gets a spicy Caribbean makeover.

TAKES 50 MINUTES • SERVES 4

4 very large potatoes
1 tbsp vegetable oil
1 red onion, ½ grated and ½ finely
  chopped
1 carrot, grated
400g/14oz minced beef
2 tsp jerk seasoning
200g/7oz fresh pineapple, finely
  chopped
1 red chilli, deseeded and finely
  chopped
small handful coriander, roughly
  chopped
juice 1 lime
lettuce leaves and burger buns,
  to serve

1 Heat oven to 190C/170C fan/gas 5.
Scrub the potatoes and cut into chips.
Lay the chips in a single layer on a baking
sheet, drizzle with oil, season and toss to
coat. Bake for 40 minutes until crisp.
2 Mix together the grated onion, carrot,
mince and jerk seasoning in a large bowl,
then shape into four evenly sized patties.
3 Heat a non-stick frying pan until hot,
then cook the burgers for 5–6 minutes
each side.
4 To make the relish, mix the chopped
red onion, pineapple, chilli, coriander and
lime juice.
5 To serve, put the burgers in split buns
with some lettuce and the spicy relish.

PER SERVING 466 kcals, protein 26g, carbs 46g,
fat 20g, sat fat 7g, fibre 5g, sugar 10g, salt 0.3g

Turkey patty & roasted root salad with Parmesan dressing

If you don't want to be left with half a celeriac, swap it for 3 parsnips, peeled and cut into batons.

TAKES 1 HOUR ● SERVES 4

3 large carrots, cut into chunky batons
1 large potato, cut into chunky batons
½ celeriac, cut into chunky batons
4 tbsp olive oil, plus extra for brushing
2 tbsp finely grated Parmesan
2 tsp white wine vinegar
1 tsp Dijon mustard
1 tbsp natural yogurt
110g bag watercress, spinach and
    rocket salad, to serve

FOR THE TURKEY PATTIES

400g/14oz minced turkey
2 tbsp torn basil leaves
1 tsp fennel seeds, crushed

1 Heat oven to 220C/200C fan/gas 7. Put the carrots, potato and celeriac in a roasting dish. Drizzle with half the olive oil and some seasoning, then cook for 45–50 minutes, turning occasionally, until tender and golden.

2 Meanwhile, make the patties. Put the mince, basil and fennel seeds in a bowl, add some seasoning and shape into little patties. Heat a griddle pan to hot, brush the patties with oil and cook for 5–6 minutes on each side, or until cooked through.

3 To make the dressing, mix the remaining oil, Parmesan, vinegar, mustard and yogurt with some seasoning. Lay the roasted veg and patties over the salad, then drizzle over the dressing and serve.

PER SERVING 393 kcals, protein 37g, carbs 24g, fat 17g, sat fat 4g, fibre 7g, sugar 9g, salt 0.6g

Spicy beef, shiitake & aubergine stir-fry

Aubergines aren't the first vegetables you think of to stir-fry, but they are delicious cooked this way and really absorb the flavours of the other ingredients.

TAKES 45 MINUTES ● SERVES 4

2 tbsp vegetable oil

500g pack extra-lean minced beef

1 large aubergine, sliced and cut into thick strips

1 red chilli, thinly sliced

6 garlic cloves, finely chopped

150g pack shiitake mushrooms, sliced

4 spring onions, halved horizontally and sliced lengthways

4 tbsp oyster sauce

1 tbsp brown sugar

cooked basmati rice, to serve

1 Heat a drop of the oil in a non-stick wok or large frying pan. Cook the mince, breaking it up with a wooden spoon, for about 10 minutes, or until cooked through. Remove with a slotted spoon and set aside.

2 Heat the remaining oil in the pan and fry the aubergine for about 10 minutes, until tender. Add half the chilli, the garlic and mushrooms, then cook for a further few minutes. Return the mince to the pan and add most of the spring onions, the oyster sauce, sugar and 200ml/7fl oz water. Bubble for a few minutes, then serve immediately with basmati rice and the remaining chilli and spring onions scattered on top.

PER SERVING 342 kcals, protein 31g, carbs 13g, fat 18g, sat fat 6g, fibre 4g, sugar 8g, salt 2.2g

Steak & onion fajitas with sweetcorn salsa

The range of Mexican ingredients that is now readily available has really grown,
so take advantage and use them in quick recipes like this one.

TAKES 35 MINUTES ● SERVES 2

1 very ripe avocado
2 limes, 1 juiced, 1 cut into wedges
100g/4oz sweetcorn from a can, or
    frozen and defrosted
1 tomato, deseeded and finely chopped
½ small bunch coriander, chopped
1 tsp garlic-infused olive oil
2 red onions, cut into wedges
140g/5oz lean beef steak, all fat
    removed and sliced
1 tbsp fajita seasoning
4 small wholemeal flour tortillas
shredded iceberg lettuce and sliced
    jalapeño peppers, to serve

1 Mash together the avocado and lime juice. Stir through the sweetcorn, tomato, half the coriander and some seasoning to make a salsa. Set aside, covered with cling film.

2 Heat the oil in a non-stick frying pan or griddle pan and cook the onions for about 8 minutes until lightly charred and slightly softened. Remove to a warmed serving dish.

3 Dust the steak with the fajita seasoning and some black pepper, then add to the pan. Cook for 2–3 minutes, depending on how rare you like it, then add to the onions. Meanwhile, warm the tortillas according to the pack instructions. Serve the steak and onions with the tortillas, salsa, lettuce, jalapeño peppers and lime wedges.

PER SERVING 594 kcals, protein 27g, carbs 69g, fat 23g, sat fat 6g, fibre 9g, sugar 12g, salt 1g

Herby pork with apple & chicory salad

A delicious way to serve a quick pork roast. The apples can be swapped for pears but make sure they are not too soft.

TAKES 35 MINUTES • SERVES 4

400g/14oz pork tenderloin, trimmed
   of any fat and sinew
1 tbsp walnut oil
2 tsp wholegrain mustard
1 tbsp each chopped tarragon and
   parsley
juice 1 lemon
1 tbsp clear honey
2 large eating apples, cored and sliced
270g pack chicory, leaves separated

1 Heat oven to 200C/180C fan/gas 6. Rub the pork with 1 teaspoon of the oil, 1 teaspoon of the mustard and some seasoning. Heat a pan and brown the pork on all sides then transfer to a baking sheet and press on half the herbs. Roast for 15 minutes until just cooked.
2 To make the salad, mix the lemon juice, honey and remaining walnut oil and mustard together. Season and toss through the apples, chicory and remaining herbs. Serve the pork sliced, with the salad on the side.

PER SERVING 215 kcals, protein 23g, carbs 15g, fat 8g, sat fat 2g, fibre 2g, sugar 14g, salt 0.3g

Light chicken korma

This lighter version of the popular korma curry delivers all the flavour but with fewer calories.

TAKES 35 MINUTES • SERVES 4

1 onion, chopped

2 garlic cloves, roughly chopped

thumb-sized piece ginger, roughly chopped

4 tbsp korma paste

4 skinless boneless chicken breasts, cut into bite-sized pieces

50g/2oz ground almonds

4 tbsp sultanas

400ml/14fl oz chicken stock

¼ tsp golden caster sugar

150g pot 0% fat thick Greek yogurt

small bunch coriander, chopped

handful of flaked almonds, to garnish (optional)

cooked white or brown basmati rice, to serve

1 Put the onion, garlic and ginger in a food processor and whizz to a paste. Tip the paste into a large high-sided frying pan with 3 tablespoons water and cook for 5 minutes. Add the korma paste and cook for a further 2 minutes until aromatic.

2 Stir the chicken into the sauce, then add the ground almonds, sultanas, stock and sugar. Give everything a good mix, then cover and simmer for 10 minutes or until the chicken is cooked through.

3 Remove the pan from the heat, stir in the yogurt and some seasoning, then scatter over the coriander and flaked almonds, if using. Serve with white or brown basmati rice.

PER SERVING 376 kcals, protein 40g, carbs 28g, fat 11g, sat fat 1g, fibre 3g, sugar 26g, salt 1.1g

Harissa chicken traybake

An easy all-in-one chicken traybake made all the more interesting with the addition of the North-African chilli paste, harissa.

TAKES 45 MINUTES ● SERVES 4

3 tbsp harissa
½ × 500g pot low-fat natural yogurt
4 skinless chicken breasts, slashed
1 small butternut squash, peeled,
  deseeded and cut into long wedges
2 red onions, cut into wedges
oil, for cooking
cooked rice or couscous, to serve

1 Heat oven to 200C/180C fan/gas 6. Mix 2 tablespoons of the harissa with 3 tablespoons of the yogurt in a small bowl. Rub all over the chicken breasts and set aside to marinate while you start the veg.

2 Toss the squash and the onions with remaining harissa, mixed with 2 tablespoons oil, and some seasoning in a large roasting tin. Roast for 10 minutes.

3 Remove the vegetables from the oven, add the chicken to the tin, then roast for a further 20–25 minutes until the chicken and veg are cooked through. Serve with the remaining yogurt on the side and a big bowl of couscous or rice.

PER SERVING 303 kcals, protein 36g, carbs 21g, fat 9g, sat fat 2g, fibre 4g, sugar 15g, salt 0.5g

Pork & green bean stir-fry

Fine green beans work best for this recipe; if they are on the bigger side you should boil them for 2 minutes and then drain them before stir-frying.

TAKES 20 MINUTES • SERVES 4

1 tbsp lime juice
1 tbsp chilli bean paste or chilli sauce
75ml/2½fl oz oyster sauce
1 tsp soy sauce
2 tbsp vegetable oil
400g/14oz pork fillet, cut into thin slices
2 garlic cloves, chopped
1 red onion, cut into chunky pieces
140g/5oz green beans, halved
steamed rice or noodles, to serve

1 In a small bowl, mix together the lime juice, chilli bean paste or sauce, oyster sauce and half the soy sauce. Set aside. Heat a large wok with 1 tablespoon of the oil. Season the pork and toss with the remaining soy sauce. Sear the meat quickly, then remove from the pan.

2 Add the remaining oil and stir-fry the garlic, onion and beans for 2 minutes. Return the meat to the pan with the chilli–lime sauce and stir-fry for another 3 minutes, until the sauce has thickened. Serve with steamed rice or noodles.

PER SERVING 233 kcals, protein 24g, carbs 7g, fat 12g, sat fat 3g, fibre 1g, sugar 5g, salt 2.42g

Salami & peppadew pizza

A pack of bread mix makes a great cheat's pizza base and means you don't have to weigh any ingredients.

TAKES 45 MINUTES • SERVES 4

500g pack bread mix

oil, for greasing

1 tbsp flour or semolina, plus extra for flouring

1 small jar pizza tomato sauce (about 150g)

100g pack sliced salami

10 peppadew peppers, halved

1 red onion, thinly sliced

large pinch crushed red chilli flakes

140g/5oz mozzarella, cut into 3cm/1¼in cubes

handful oregano, leaves picked

1 Heat oven to 220C/200C fan/gas 7. Mix the bread dough according to the pack instructions. Knead the dough for a few minutes, then put in a covered, oiled bowl and leave at room temperature for 30 minutes to rise.

2 Take the dough and squash it to knock out the air. Roll out on a floured surface to fit the largest baking sheet you have. Sprinkle flour or semolina over the baking sheet, then put the dough on top. Spread the tomato sauce over the dough, then scatter with the salami, peppadews, onion, chilli flakes, mozzarella and oregano. Bake for 12–15 minutes or until the dough turns crusty and golden.

PER SERVING 612 kcals, protein 25g, carbs 82g, fat 22g, sat fat 9g, fibre 8g, sugar 11g, salt 4.82g

Herby toad in the hole

For best results, get the fat as hot as possible before adding the batter, and don't peep in the oven during the first 25 minutes of cooking.

TAKES 50 MINUTES • SERVES 4

140g/5oz plain flour
3 eggs
300ml/½ pint milk
2 tsp Dijon mustard
2 tbsp vegetable oil
8 Cumberland sausages
8 sage leaves
4 rosemary sprigs

1 Heat oven to 240C/220C fan/gas 9. In a food processor, combine the flour, eggs, milk, mustard and some salt and pepper, blitz until smooth, then leave to rest for 30 minutes.

2 Pour the oil into a metal roasting tin about 30 × 23cm and 7.5cm deep. Brush the oil all over the sides and bottom, then put in the oven. When the oil in the roasting tin is very hot and smoking, add the sausages to the tin, evenly spread out, and cook for 5 minutes.

3 Give the rested batter a stir and pour into the really hot tin – take care as it may spit. Quickly sprinkle over the sage leaves and rosemary, then put in the middle of the oven. Do not open the door for 25 minutes, then check to see if the batter is puffed up and brown and completely cooked through. If needed, cook for a further 5–10 minutes. Serve straight from the dish.

PER SERVING 552 kcals, protein 28g, carbs 40g, fat 32g, sat fat 10g, fibre 1g, sugar 5g, salt 1.90g

Baked fennel pork with lemony potatoes & onions

This all-in-one pot roast would also work with chicken breasts or chunky white fish fillets.

TAKES 1 HOUR ● SERVES 4

2 tbsp fennel seeds

1 tbsp olive oil

4 pork loin steaks, trimmed of fat

1 large onion, sliced

2 garlic cloves, thinly sliced

750g/1lb 10oz baby new potatoes,
   halved lengthways

2 fennel bulbs, thinly sliced, green
   fronds reserved

juice 2 lemons

350g/12oz broccoli, broken into florets

1 Crush the fennel seeds lightly in a pestle and mortar. Mix with half the oil and a little seasoning. Rub into the pork and set aside.

2 Heat oven to 200C/180C fan/gas 6. Heat the remaining oil in a shallow ovenproof dish with a lid. Soften the onion and garlic for about 5 minutes, then tip in the potatoes and brown for a few minutes. Add the fennel, lemon juice and about 100ml/3½fl oz water. Season, cover with the lid and cook in the oven for 35 minutes.

3 Remove the lid, stir the potatoes and place the meat on top. Return to the oven, uncovered, and cook for another 10 minutes or until the pork is cooked to your liking. Meanwhile, cook the broccoli.

4 Scatter over the reserved fennel fronds and serve with the broccoli.

PER SERVING 407 kcals, protein 40g, carbs 40g, fat 11g, sat fat 3g, fibre 7g, sugar 8g, salt 0.33g

Swede & potato rösti-topped shepherd's pie

A firm family favourite with a new-style crispy topping – any leftovers can be frozen.

TAKES 1¾ HOURS • SERVES 5

500g/1lb 2oz swede, peeled and cut into large chunks

500g/1lb 2oz floury potatoes, peeled and left whole

1 tbsp olive oil

1 onion, chopped

2 carrots, chopped

250g/9oz mushrooms, quartered

500g/1lb 2oz minced lamb

400g can tomatoes

2 tbsp tomato purée

50g/2oz butter, melted

1 Cook the swede and potatoes in a pan of boiling salted water for 10 minutes until tender, then drain and set aside.

2 Heat oven to 200C/180C fan/gas 6. Heat the oil in a large frying pan over a low heat. Add the onion and carrots, and gently fry for 5 minutes. Add the mushrooms, increase the heat to medium and cook for a further 5 minutes. Tip the vegetables into a bowl.

3 Add the mince to the frying pan and cook until browned. Pour away any excess fat then add the fried vegetables (not the swede and potatoes), tomatoes and tomato purée, cover and simmer for 15 minutes, topping up with a little water if the mince looks a bit dry.

4 When the swede and potatoes are cool enough to handle, coarsely grate then toss in the melted butter and season.

5 Tip the mince mixture into a deep ovenproof dish, top with the grated swede and potatoes, then put in the oven and cook for 40 minutes until brown and bubbling.

PER SERVING 542 kcals, protein 31g, carbs 35g, fat 31g, sat fat 15g, fibre 7g, sugar 15g, salt 0.7g

Lamb & apricot stew

Ras-el-hanout is a spice blend from Morocco. If you can't find it then you can use the more readily available Indian spice mix, garam masala, instead.

TAKES 45 MINUTES ● SERVES 2

2 tbsp olive oil
250g/9oz stewing lamb pieces
1 onion, thinly sliced
1 garlic clove, chopped
1 tbsp chopped ginger
2 tsp ras-el-hanout spice mix
1 tbsp tomato purée
5 soft dried apricots, halved
300ml/½ pint vegetable or chicken
    stock
mint or coriander leaves, and lemon
    wedges, to garnish
couscous, to serve

1 In a medium-sized pan, heat 1 tablespoon of the oil. Season the meat and fry briefly until browned. Transfer the meat from the pan and add the remaining oil. Add the onion, garlic and ginger, and fry with a little seasoning. Cook for 5 minutes until soft, then add the spice mix, tomato purée, apricots and stock, and return the lamb to the pan.

2 Simmer gently for 25 minutes then serve with warm couscous, and a garnish of mint or coriander leaves, and lemon wedges.

PER SERVING 447 kcals, protein 32g, carbs 19g, fat 28g, sat fat 10g, fibre 4g, sugar 15g, salt 0.69g

Cottage pie cakes

This homely supper makes a whole new meal out of leftover mashed potato.

TAKES 35 MINUTES • MAKES 6

400g/14oz pack lean minced beef
1 beef stock cube
50g/2oz plain flour
2 tbsp Worcestershire sauce
140g/5oz frozen peas
450g/1lb leftover mashed potatoes
2 eggs, beaten
85g/3oz dried breadcrumbs
vegetable oil, for frying
baked beans, to serve

1 Heat a large frying pan until hot. Dry-fry the mince until browned, breaking it up with a fork. Crumble in the stock cube and 1 tablespoon of the flour, and mix well. Add the Worcestershire sauce and peas, and mix well to combine.
2 Tip the mince mixture into a bowl and cool a little, before stirring in the mash and shaping into six cakes. Dust the cakes in the remaining flour, then dip them into the egg, then the crumbs. Chill for at least 10 minutes, longer if you have time.
3 Heat the oil in a large pan. Fry the cakes for 3–4 minutes each side, until golden brown. Drain on kitchen paper. Season with a little salt and serve with baked beans.

PER SERVING 426 kcals, protein 23g, carbs 31g, fat 25g, sat fat 7g, fibre 3g, sugar 2g, salt 1.22g

Sloppy Joe's pizza breads

Using French bread as quick cheat's pizza base gives you a delicious doughy middle with a crusty underside.

TAKES 30 MINUTES ● SERVES 4

500g pack lean minced beef
350g jar tomato and chilli pasta sauce
1 French stick, split lengthways
2 × 125g balls mozzarella, drained
    and torn
small handful basil, torn
salad leaves, to serve

1 Cook the mince in a large pan over a medium heat for 8 minutes, until browned. Pour in the tomato and chilli sauce and leave to bubble, uncovered, for 15 minutes until thickened. Season to taste.

2 Heat the grill. Cut the French stick halves into two pieces. Put the bread cut-side up on a baking sheet and grill for 2–3 minutes to lightly toast. Remove from the grill and divide the mince among the bread. Scatter over the mozzarella.

3 Grill for 3–4 minutes more, until the cheese is bubbling and golden. Scatter with basil and serve with a salad.

PER SERVING 618 kcals, protein 48g, carbs 45g, fat 27g, sat fat 14g, fibre 2.5g, sugar 7g, salt 3g

Keema curry & raita

You can't beat making your own curry paste for freshness of flavour, but if you are pushed for time then a shop-bought korma paste will do fine.

TAKES 40 MINUTES • SERVES 4

1 onion, chopped
400g/14oz lean minced beef
350g/12oz frozen peas
handful coriander leaves, chopped
brown rice, to serve (optional)

FOR THE PASTE

1 green chilli, deseeded and chopped
2 garlic cloves, chopped
thumb-sized piece ginger, chopped
½ tsp each ground turmeric and
    coriander
1 tbsp korma curry powder

FOR THE RAITA

200g/7oz fat-free natural yogurt
100g/4oz cucumber, peeled, deseeded
    and diced
handful fresh mint, chopped

1 Whizz together the ingredients for the paste in a blender or food processor – add a splash of water, if you need to.
2 Cook the onion in a splash of water for about 5 minutes until softened. Stir in the mince and cook for another 5 minutes to brown. Add the paste, cook for 1 minute, then pour in 100ml/3½fl oz water. Bring to the boil and simmer for 15 minutes.
3 Meanwhile, mix together the raita ingredients and season to taste. When the mince is cooked, season and stir through the coriander leaves. Serve with the raita and some brown rice, if you like.

PER SERVING 289 kcals, protein 31g, carbs 17g, fat 11g, sat fat 5g, fibre 5g, sugar 8g, salt 0.39g

Tandoori prawn skewers with rice & chopped salad

If you're using wooden skewers for these tasty kebabs, make sure you soak them in water for 20 minutes first to stop them burning.

TAKES 25 MINUTES • SERVES 2

100g/4oz thick Greek yogurt
juice ½ lime, other ½ cut into 2 wedges
½ tsp each curry powder and hot paprika
1 tsp grated ginger
½ small pack coriander, roughly chopped
200g/7oz large peeled raw prawns
100g/4oz basmati rice
¼ cucumber, deseeded and sliced
100g/4oz cherry tomatoes, halved
½ small red onion, cut into thin half moons
½ tbsp sunflower oil

1 Scoop half the yogurt into a bowl. Add the lime juice, spices, ginger and 1 tablespoon of the coriander. Season, mix well, then add the prawns and set aside.

2 Cook the rice according to the pack instructions. Mix together the cucumber, tomatoes, onion and some seasoning.

3 Thread half the prawns on to skewers. Heat the oil in a griddle pan or large, wide pan. Griddle the prawn skewers for 1 minute on each side or until they turn opaque.

4 Serve the salad with the prawn skewers, rice and remaining yogurt, and the lime wedges for squeezing over. Sprinkle with the remaining coriander.

PER SERVING 436 kcals, protein 27g, carbs 53g, fat 10g, sat fat 5g, fibre 1g, sugar 6g, salt 0.6g

Miso pollack with cucumber & spring onion salad

If you can't find miso paste then up the amount of soy sauce to 2 tablespoons and also add a large pinch of caster sugar.

TAKES 25 MINUTES • SERVES 2

2 tbsp white miso paste

1 tsp low-sodium soy sauce

4 tbsp rice wine vinegar

2 skinless pollack fillets, about 125g/4½oz each

1 bunch spring onions, sliced diagonally

½ cucumber, peeled into strips with a potato peeler

140g/5oz beansprouts

100g/4oz radishes, sliced

1 red chilli, chopped (deseeded, if you like)

3 limes, 2 juiced, 1 cut into wedges

1 tsp sesame oil

1 Mix together the miso paste, soy sauce and half the vinegar. Cover the fish in the marinade and leave for at least 15 minutes, or ideally overnight in the fridge.

2 Mix the spring onions, cucumber, beansprouts and radishes. Make a dressing with the chilli, lime juice and remaining vinegar. Pour over the vegetables and set aside while you cook the fish.

3 Heat the sesame oil in a frying pan and cook the fish for 3–4 minutes each side. Remove and transfer to a plate. Tip the marinade into the pan, bring to the boil and boil rapidly to reduce by half. Pour over the fish and serve with the vegetable salad and lime wedges to squeeze over.

PER SERVING 250 kcals, protein 26g, carbs 24g, fat 4g, sat fat 1g, fibre 4g, sugar 17g, salt 1.5g

Oven-baked fish & chips

This healthy makeover means you don't have to miss out on one of the nation's favourite suppers.

TAKES 55 MINUTES • SERVES 4

800g/1lb 12oz floury potatoes, scrubbed and cut into chips
2 tbsp olive oil
50g/2oz fresh breadcrumbs
zest 1 lemon
2 tbsp chopped flat-leaf parsley
4 thick sustainable white fish fillets (about 140g/5oz each)
200g/7oz cherry tomatoes

1 Heat oven to 220C/200C fan/gas 7. Pat the chips dry on kitchen paper, then lay in a single layer on a large baking sheet. Drizzle with half the olive oil and season with salt. Cook for 40 minutes, turning after 20 minutes, so they cook evenly.

2 Mix the breadcrumbs with the lemon zest and parsley, then season well. Top the cod evenly with the breadcrumb mixture, then drizzle with the remaining oil. Put in a roasting tin with the cherry tomatoes, then bake in the oven for the final 10 minutes of the chips' cooking time.

PER SERVING 366 kcals, protein 32g, carbs 43g, fat 7g, sat fat 1g, fibre 4g, sugar 3g, salt 0.5g

Oaty fish & prawn gratins

A new, healthier and quicker take on fish pie – without compromising any of its comfort factor.

TAKES 40 MINUTES • MAKES 2

340g bag baby leaf spinach, roughly
    chopped
400g can chopped tomatoes with garlic
    and herbs
225g/8oz sustainable white fish fillets,
    chopped into large chunks
small bunch basil, torn
100g/4oz cooked peeled prawns
2 tbsp finely grated Parmesan
2 tbsp breadcrumbs
2 tbsp oats
175g/6oz broccoli, boiled or steamed,
    to serve

1 Put the spinach in a large colander and pour over boiling water. Once cool enough to handle, squeeze out any excess water, then season.

2 Tip the tomatoes into a frying pan with some seasoning and simmer for 5 minutes. Add the fish and heat for 1–2 minutes – it doesn't need to be fully cooked at this point. Stir in the basil.

3 Heat oven to 220C/200C fan/gas 7. Divide the spinach, fish, prawns and tomato sauce between two gratin dishes. Mix the Parmesan, breadcrumbs and oats together and sprinkle over the top. Bake for 20 minutes until golden and bubbling. Serve with the broccoli.

PER SERVING 359 kcals, protein 48g, carbs 27g, fat 6g, sat fat 2g, fibre 8g, sugar 9g, salt 3.4g

Tuna & sweetcorn slice

Using ready-rolled puff pastry is a real time-saver on a weeknight and saves you all the mess of getting flour everywhere.

TAKES 35 MINUTES • SERVES 4

320g pack ready-rolled puff pastry
185g can tuna in spring water, drained
    and flaked
325g can sweetcorn, drained
3 tbsp crème fraîche
50g/2oz Cheddar, grated
a few chives, snipped into 1cm/½in
    lengths, to sprinkle

1 Heat oven to 220C/200C fan/ gas 7. Lay the pastry out on a baking sheet. Pinch up the edges to form a border, pressing firmly into the corners. Prick the centre all over with a fork and pop in the oven for 10–15 minutes.

2 Meanwhile, mix the tuna and sweetcorn in a bowl, and season.

3 Remove the pastry from the oven, pressing the centre down with the back of a fork, as it will have puffed up a bit. Spread the crème fraîche across the centre, spoon the tuna mix on top, then sprinkle over the cheese. Bake for 10–15 minutes more, until golden, puffed up and cooked through. Sprinkle with chives and cut into quarters to serve.

PER SERVING 463 kcals, protein 18g, carbs 29g, fat 30g, sat fat 16g, fibre 1g, sugar 2g, salt 2.6g

Salmon & broccoli cakes with watercress salad

Broccoli makes a welcome addition to these chunky fishcakes. If you're cooking for two, still make four as they freeze well.

TAKES 30 MINUTES ● **SERVES 4**

500g/1lb 2oz potatoes, cut into chunks
85g/3oz broccoli, cut into small florets
pack of 2 poached salmon fillets
juice 1 lemon, plus extra wedges to garnish
small bunch dill, chopped
1 tbsp sunflower oil
1 tbsp Dijon mustard
1 avocado, peeled, stoned and roughly chopped
100g/4oz cherry tomatoes, halved
100g bag watercress

1 Cover the potatoes in salted water, bring to the boil and simmer for 8–10 minutes, until just tender, adding the broccoli 3 minutes before the end of cooking time. Drain, allow it all to steam-dry, then roughly mash in the salmon, half the lemon juice, the dill and some seasoning, then shape into four cakes.

2 Heat the oil in a pan and fry the cakes for 3 minutes each side until golden. Meanwhile, mix the remaining lemon juice with the mustard and some seasoning to make a dressing, then set aside.

3 Mix the avocado, tomatoes and watercress, and divide among plates. Serve one fishcake each with the salad, drizzled with dressing, and with extra lemon wedges for squeezing over.

PER SERVING 315 kcals, protein 17g, carbs 23g, fat 18g, sat fat 3g, fibre 4g, sugar 3g, salt 0.7g

Quick prawn, coconut & tomato curry

This one-pan curry in a hurry can also be made with diced chicken breast, but you would need to simmer it for a few minutes longer than the prawns.

TAKES 30 MINUTES • SERVES 4

2 tbsp vegetable oil
1 medium onion, thinly sliced
2 garlic cloves, sliced
1 green chilli, deseeded and sliced
3 tbsp Thai red curry paste
1 tbsp tomato purée
200ml/7fl oz vegetable stock
200ml/7fl oz coconut cream
350g/12oz raw prawns
coriander sprigs, to garnish
steamed or boiled rice, to serve

1 Heat the oil in a large frying pan. Fry the onion, garlic and half the chilli for 5 minutes or until softened. Add the curry paste and cook for 1 minute more. Add the tomato purée, stock and coconut cream.

2 Simmer on a medium heat for 10 minutes, then add the prawns. Cook for 3 minutes or until they turn opaque. Scatter on the remaining green chilli and coriander sprigs, then serve with rice.

PER SERVING 335 kcals, protein 19g, carbs 7g, fat 26g, sat fat 16g, fibre 1g, sugar 6g, salt 1.03g

Pepper lime salmon with blackeye beans

In just half an hour you can make this impressive but easy meal for two that needs nothing else serving with it.

TAKES 30 MINUTES • SERVES 2

2 salmon fillets (about 125g/4½oz each)
1 tbsp Creole or Cajun seasoning mix
100g/4oz basmati rice
400g can blackeye beans, rinsed
    and drained
1 tbsp hot pepper sauce
1 tbsp clear honey
2 limes, 1 juiced, 1 cut into wedges
small bunch coriander, roughly
    chopped, plus extra to scatter

1 Heat the grill to hot. Roll the salmon in the spicy seasoning mix to cover. Cook the basmati rice according to the pack instructions, adding the blackeye beans for the final 2 minutes of cooking. Drain, put back in the pan and cover with a lid and set aside.

2 Grill the salmon fillets for about 8 minutes without turning. While they cook, mix together the pepper sauce, honey and lime juice.

3 Stir the coriander through the rice, drizzle the sauce over the salmon, scatter with extra coriander leaves, and serve with the lime wedges to squeeze over.

PER SERVING 581 kcals, protein 41g, carbs 67g, fat 16g, sat fat 3g, fibre 8g, sugar 10g, salt 0.6g

Steamed tilapia with green chilli & coconut chutney

If you haven't tried tilapia it's a meaty white fish that is now readily available from supermarkets and works really well in spiced dishes.

TAKES 20 MINUTES • SERVES 2

100g/4oz basmati rice
2 large tilapia fillets
2 tsp butter
fat-free yogurt and small naan breads, to serve

FOR THE CHUTNEY

handful coriander, roughly chopped
½ green chilli, deseeded
25g/1oz desiccated coconut
1 lemon, ½ juiced, ½ cut in wedges
1 tsp chopped ginger
½ tsp ground cumin
good pinch of sugar

1 To make the chutney, put the coriander, chilli, coconut, lemon juice, ginger and cumin in a food processor. Add good pinches of salt and sugar, then pulse to a rough salsa-like consistency.

2 Rinse the rice and put in a deep frying pan with a lid, with 225ml/8fl oz water. Bring to the boil, then turn down low – it will take about 8 minutes to cook.

3 After about 3 minutes, put the fish fillets on top of the rice, then dot a teaspoon of butter on each and spread the fresh chutney over in a thick layer. Cover with a lid and cook over a low heat for about 5 minutes until the fish and rice are cooked through.

4 Serve the fish and rice with the yogurt, warmed naan breads and the lemon wedges to squeeze over.

PER SERVING 418 kcals, protein 32g, carbs 42g, fat 15g, sat fat 10g, fibre 2g, sugar 2g, salt 0.28g

Grilled mackerel with soy, lime & ginger

Not only is this a good-looking main meal, it's also high in healthy omega 3 fatty acids.

TAKES 25 MINUTES ● SERVES 2

300g/10oz mackerel
100g/4oz jasmine rice
4 spring onions, sliced
1 red pepper, deseeded and diced

FOR THE MARINADE

1 tbsp low-sodium soy sauce
juice 1 lime
small piece fresh ginger, grated
1 garlic clove, crushed
2 tbsp clear honey

1 To make the marinade, mix all the ingredients together and pour over the mackerel. Cover and chill for 30 minutes.
2 Heat grill and put the mackerel, skin-side up, on a baking sheet lined with foil. Grill for 5 minutes, then turn and baste with remaining marinade. Grill for 5 minutes more.
3 Cook the rice according to the pack instructions, then drain and toss with the spring onions and pepper. Serve with the mackerel.

PER SERVING 587 kcals, protein 33g, carbs 61g, fat 25g, sat fat 5g, fibre 1g, sugar 17g, salt 1.1g

Smoked trout fish pies

Swap the trout for hot-smoked salmon, or a mixture of prawns with some snipped smoked salmon trimmings.

TAKES 35 MINUTES • SERVES 4

1½ tbsp butter
3 tbsp flour
350ml/12fl oz full-fat milk
1–2 tbsp creamed horseradish
   (optional)
small bunch dill, chopped
large bunch spring onions, chopped
zest 1 lemon
2 × 175g packs smoked trout fillets,
   any skin removed, flaked into big
   chunks
450g/1lb leftover mashed potato

1 Heat oven to 200C/180C fan/gas 6. Melt the butter in a pan, then stir in the flour for 1 minute. Gradually stir in the milk and horseradish, if using. Bubble the sauce to thicken for a couple of minutes, then add the dill, three-quarters of the onions, the lemon zest, fish and some seasoning. Pour into four individual pie dishes or one large pie dish.
2 Mix the mashed potato with the remaining spring onions, spoon over the fish mixture, then bake for 15–20 minutes until golden and bubbling and serve.

PER SERVING 382 kcals, protein 27g, carbs 27g, fat 19g, sat fat 6g, fibre 3g, sugar 6g, salt 2.58g

Mediterranean fish & couscous

Cooking fish in a foil parcel locks in all the flavour and means you get to keep all the tasty cooking juices too.

TAKES 30 MINUTES • SERVES 2

2 sustainable white fish fillets (we used pollack), about 125g/4½oz each

2 lemons, zest and juice of 1, the other cut into wedges

1 red chilli, half sliced, half finely chopped

small bunch basil, torn

200g/7oz cherry tomatoes

100g/4oz couscous

2 tbsp balsamic vinegar

½ cucumber, diced

2 tbsp pitted black olives, halved

1 Heat oven to 200C/180C fan/gas 6. Take one small sheet of foil, about A4 size, and put one fish fillet on top. Season the fish, then drizzle with a quarter of the lemon juice and zest, half the sliced chilli and half of the basil.

2 Halve four of the tomatoes and put these around the fish. Put another sheet of foil on top and fold the edges together to seal. Repeat with the other piece of fish and transfer to a baking sheet. Cook for 15–18 minutes until the bag has puffed up (or cook on the barbecue).

3 While the fish is cooking pour 100ml/3½fl oz of boiling water over the couscous, cover, then leave to swell for 5 minutes. Chop the rest of the tomatoes and mix with the couscous, balsamic, cucumber, the remaining basil, lemon juice and zest and the olives. Season and serve alongside the fish with the lemon wedges on the side for squeezing over.

PER SERVING 263 kcals, protein 26g, carbs 34g, fat 4g, sat fat 1g, fibre 2g, sugar 9g, salt 0.52g

Crisp spiced fish fingers

Making your own fish fingers is healthier than eating bought ones and means you can include other elements like spices or herbs.

TAKES 25 MINUTES • SERVES 2

300g/10oz chunky skinless haddock fillet
2 tsp cornflour
2 tsp polenta
3 tbsp sunflower oil
½ red chilli, finely sliced
12 basil leaves, torn, plus a few extra leaves to garnish
3 tbsp soy sauce
juice ½ lime, plus lime wedges to squeeze over
100g/4oz Thai fragrant rice

1 Cut the fish into pieces about 5 × 10cm/2 × 4in. Pat dry with some kitchen towel. Mix the cornflour and polenta on a plate and season with salt and pepper. Add the haddock and turn to coat in the mixture.
2 Heat 2 tablespoons of the oil in a large frying pan and add the haddock fingers. Cook for 5–8 minutes, turning occasionally. Remove from the pan and drain on kitchen paper. Keep warm.
3 Wipe out the pan with kitchen towel. Return to the heat and add the remaining oil. Add the chilli and cook for 1 minute, then remove from the heat and add the basil, soy and lime juice to make a spicy sauce.
4 Cook the rice for 10–12 minutes, until tender. Drain well and serve with the haddock fingers, spicy sauce, lime wedges and a few basil leaves.

PER SERVING 309 kcals, protein 30g, carbs 9g, fat 18g, sat fat 2g, fibre none, sugar 2g, salt 4.33g

Cajun spiced salmon

Perfect for someone on a low-salt diet, this dish is highly flavoured without needing any extra seasoning.

TAKES 25 MINUTES • SERVES 2

2 salmon fillets (about 140g/5oz each)
juice 1 lime
pinch chilli powder
½ tsp ground cumin
½ tsp smoked paprika
½ tsp ground coriander
pinch soft brown sugar
sunflower oil, for greasing
steamed rice, to serve

FOR THE SALSA

1 ripe avocado, peeled and diced
handful cherry tomatoes, quartered
2 spring onions, sliced
juice 1 lime
splash of olive oil
bunch coriander, half roughly chopped,
   half picked into sprigs

1 Put the salmon in a bowl, pour over the lime juice and leave to cure for 5 minutes. Meanwhile, mix all the spices together with the sugar. Lift the salmon out of the lime juice and roll each fillet in the spicy sugar so they are both completely coated.

2 Heat grill to high. Grease a baking sheet, then sit the salmon, flesh-side up, on the sheet. Grill for 5 minutes, until the fish is cooked through and the edges are starting to blacken. While the salmon is cooking, gently mix all the salsa ingredients together with the roughly chopped coriander.

3 When the fish is cooked, serve with the salsa, some rice and the coriander sprigs scattered over.

PER SERVING 463 kcals, protein 31g, carbs 5g, fat 36g, sat fat 7g, fibre 3g, sugar 3g, salt 0.21g

Curry-crusted fish

These fish fillets freeze really well raw with their topping, as long as the fish hasn't been previously frozen.

TAKES 15 MINUTES ● SERVES 4

3 slices bread (about 85g/3oz total)
1 tbsp korma curry paste
4 thick white fish fillets
1 lime

1 Heat oven to 200C/180C fan/gas 6. Put the bread into the bowl of a food processor and whizz until you have rough crumbs. Add the curry paste and whizz again until the crumbs are fairly fine and evenly coated in the paste.
2 Put the fish fillets on to a baking sheet, season on both sides, then grate the zest of half the lime on top of each fillet. Gently press the curry-paste crumbs on top of the fish, then bake until the fish is cooked through and the topping crisp and golden, about 7 minutes.

PER SERVING 178 kcals, protein 29g, carbs 11g, fat 2g, sat fat none, fibre none, sugar 1g, salt 0.64g

Pan-fried mackerel with orange salsa

The orange salsa is easy to make and its punchiness is the perfect foil for oily fish such as mackerel or salmon.

TAKES 20 MINUTES • **SERVES 2**

4 mackerel fillets (about 75g/2½oz
  each)
½ tsp smoked paprika
2 oranges, segmented
1 large shallot, very finely sliced
50g/2oz pitted Kalamata olives, roughly
  chopped
½ 20g pack flat-leaf parsley, chopped
1 tbsp olive oil
new potatoes and green beans,
  to serve (optional)

1 Rub the fish fillets on both sides with the paprika and a little salt, then set aside. Mix the orange segments in a small bowl with the shallot, olives, parsley and a good grinding of black pepper to make the salsa.

2 Heat the oil in a large frying pan and fry the mackerel on both sides for 2–3 minutes. Serve with the orange salsa and some new potatoes and green beans, if you like.

PER SERVING 466 kcals, protein 30g, carbs 10g, fat 34g, sat fat 6g, fibre 3g, sugar 10g, salt 1.3g

Soy & ginger salmon with soba noodles

The same recipe can be applied to any fish fillets, but mackerel would also work particularly well.

TAKES 25 MINUTES ● SERVES 4

thumb-sized piece ginger, peeled and
   finely chopped

1 garlic clove, finely chopped

6 tbsp light soy sauce

4 tbsp rice wine vinegar

4 salmon fillets (about 140g/5oz each)

200g/7oz soba noodles

350g/12oz frozen soya beans,
   defrosted

2 × 175g packs baby corn and
   mangetout mix, chopped

1 In a small bowl, mix the ginger, garlic, soy and vinegar. Add the salmon and leave to marinate for 10 minutes. Heat a large non-stick frying pan. Lift the fish from the marinade with a slotted spoon, reserving the marinade, and fry for 2–3 minutes on each side, then tip in the marinade and a splash of water and bubble for 1 minute.

2 Cook the noodles according to the pack instructions. Tip in the soya beans 3 minutes before the end, then add the veg mix for the final minute. Drain everything really well. Serve the noodles and veg with the salmon and sauce spooned over.

PER SERVING 531 kcals, protein 48g, carbs 32g, fat 22g, sat fat 4g, fibre 7g, sugar 9g, salt 2.2g

Cod with bacon, lettuce & peas

Cooked lettuce is delicious but it literally needs only a few minutes on the heat, or it will lose all its texture.

TAKES 20 MINUTES ● SERVES 2

2 tsp sunflower oil

2 rashers rindless smoked streaky bacon, cut into small pieces

1 long shallot or small onion, very finely sliced

1 garlic clove, crushed

2 thick skinless cod fillets, (about 140g/5oz each)

140g/5oz frozen peas

200ml/7fl oz chicken stock, fresh or made with ½ stock cube

2 Little Gem lettuces, thickly shredded

2 tbsp half-fat crème fraîche

thick slices crusty wholegrain bread, to serve

1 Heat the oil in a medium non-stick frying pan. Add the bacon, shallot or onion and garlic. Cook gently, stirring, for 2 minutes, then push to one side of the pan.

2 Season the cod with ground black pepper. Fry in the pan for 2 minutes, then turn over. Add the peas and stock, and bring to a simmer. Cook over a medium heat for a further 2 minutes, then add the lettuces and crème fraîche. Cook for a couple of minutes more, stirring the vegetables occasionally, until the fish is just cooked and the lettuce has wilted. Serve with bread to mop up the broth.

PER SERVING 430 kcals, protein 42g, carbs 32g, fat 15g, sat fat 5g, fibre 7g, sugar 5g, salt 1.8g

Chocolate & raspberry pots

This pudding is easy enough for children to make – just get an adult to melt the chocolate.

TAKES 25 MINUTES ● SERVES 6

200g/7oz dark chocolate
100g/4oz raspberries
500g/1lb 2oz thick Greek yogurt
3 tbsp clear honey
chocolate curls or sprinkles, to
    decorate

1 Break the chocolate into small pieces and put in a heatproof bowl. Bring a little water to the boil in a small pan, then put the bowl of chocolate on top, making sure the bottom of the bowl does not touch the water. Leave the chocolate to melt slowly over a low heat.

2 Remove the chocolate from the heat and leave to cool for 10 minutes. Meanwhile, divide the raspberries among six small ramekins or glasses.

3 When the chocolate has cooled slightly, quickly mix in the yogurt and honey. Spoon the chocolate mixture over the raspberries. Put in the fridge to cool, then finish the pots with a few chocolate curls or sprinkles before serving.

PER SERVING 320 kcals, protein 7g, carbs 33g, fat 18g, sat fat 11g, fibre 1g, sugar 33g, salt 0.1g

Banoffee mess

As there is no cooking and you don't have to worry about these desserts looking neat, this is a great recipe for kids to make.

TAKES 10 MINUTES ● SERVES 6

300ml pot double cream

6 meringue nests

5–6 sliced bananas

5 tbsp toffee sauce, plus extra to
  drizzle

handful roughly broken pecan nuts

1 Lightly whip the double cream in a large bowl, then crumble in the meringue nests. Carefully fold in the sliced bananas (use 5 or 6 depending on size) and swirl in the toffee sauce.
2 Spoon into the six dishes, then scatter over a handful of the pecan nuts and drizzle with a little more toffee sauce.

PER SERVING 446 kcals, protein 4g, carbs 49g, fat 27g, sat fat 14g, fibre 1g, sugar 21g, salt 0.13g

Easy vanilla cheesecake

All the flavour of cheesecake without any cooking or any hassle whatsoever.

TAKES 15 MINUTES • MAKES 2

4 shortbread biscuits
300g tub soft cheese
zest and juice 1 lime
3 tbsp icing sugar
380g pack frozen mixed berries

1 Put the shortbread biscuits into a plastic bag and bash with a rolling pin until broken. Divide between two dessert glasses. Beat together the soft cheese with the zest of a lime and 2 tablespoons of the icing sugar until smooth. Put this on top of each biscuit base and smooth out with the back of a spoon.

2 Take the mixed frozen berries, defrost and blend half with the remaining tablespoon of icing sugar and the juice of the lime. Pour this on top of each cheesecake and scatter with the reserved whole berries. Serve immediately or leave in the fridge for a few hours before serving.

PER CHEESECAKE 681 kcals, protein 12g, carbs 55g, fat 48g, sat fat 35g, fibre 4g, sugar 35g, salt 1.85g

Pineapple with lime & vanilla syrup

You can also add a bashed lemongrass stalk to the syrup – just remove it before drizzling the syrup over the pineapple.

TAKES 20 MINUTES • SERVES 6

100g/4oz caster sugar

1 tsp vanilla paste

juice 1 lime

1 pineapple, peeled and very thinly sliced

vanilla or coconut ice cream, to serve (optional)

1 Gently heat the caster sugar, vanilla paste, lime juice and 50ml/2fl oz water in a pan until the sugar dissolves.

2 Arrange the pineapple over a plate or platter. Drizzle over the syrup and set aside until ready to serve so the syrup can soak into the pineapple. Eat with vanilla or coconut ice cream, if you like.

PER SERVING 119 kcals, protein none, carbs 31g, fat none, sat fat none, fibre 2g, sugar 31g, salt 0.01g

Balsamic blueberries with vanilla ice cream

Poaching blueberries really brings out their flavour, especially with a dash of balsamic vinegar. Serve warm or cold over good-quality shop-bought ice cream.

TAKES 15 MINUTES • SERVES 2

125g/4½oz blueberries
1 tbsp caster sugar
1 tsp balsamic vinegar
4 scoops good-quality vanilla ice cream
   and crisp biscuits, to serve

1 Tip the blueberries into a pan with the sugar, vinegar and 1 tablespoon water. Heat very gently for 1–2 minutes until the berries soften, but don't let them burst. Set aside until ready to serve.

2 Spoon over the ice cream and eat with crisp biscuits.

PER SERVING (without biscuits) 262 kcals, protein 5g, carbs 36g, fat 12g, sat fat 8g, fibre 1g, sugar 35g, salt 0.19g

Easiest-ever pancakes

This recipe couldn't be simpler. Make up the batter, add melted butter, and your mix will make delicious thick pancakes ready to serve with your favourite filling.

TAKES 25 MINUTES ● MAKES 12

FOR THE BASIC BATTER
140g/5oz plain flour
4 eggs
200ml/7fl oz milk
50g/2oz butter, melted
sunflower oil, for frying

1 To make the batter, tip the flour into a bowl and beat in the eggs until smooth. Gradually add the milk and carry on beating until the mix is completely lump-free.

2 Now whisk in the melted butter. Put a pancake pan over a medium heat and wipe with oiled kitchen paper. Ladle some batter into the pan, tilting the pan to move the mix around the pan and pour off any excess. Cook for about 30 seconds until golden, then flip over and cook on the other side.

3 Pile the pancakes up and serve with your favourite filling.

PER PANCAKE 209 kcals, protein 4g, carbs 10g, fat 17g, sat fat 4g, fibre none, sugar 1g, salt 0.14g

Lemon syllabub

Try using half 0% fat Greek yogurt and half cream to create a healthier dessert.

TAKES 10 MINUTES • SERVES 4
284ml pot whipping cream
50g/2oz caster sugar
50ml/2fl oz white wine
zest and juice ½ lemon
almond thins or berries, to serve

1 Whip the cream and sugar together until soft peaks form. Stir in the wine, most of the lemon zest and all the juice.
2 Spoon into four glasses or bowls, sprinkle with the remaining zest and serve with almond thins or berries.

PER SERVING 328 kcals, protein 2g, carbs 15g, fat 29g, sat fat 18g, fibre none, sugar 15g, salt 0.05g

Sticky sultana pudding

This is best eaten straight away – as it only takes 5 minutes to cook, you can make it just before you need it.

TAKES 10 MINUTES ● SERVES 4–6

100g/4oz butter, plus extra for the basin
200g/7oz plain flour
1 tsp baking powder
85g/3oz light muscovado sugar
100g/4oz sultanas
2 large eggs, lightly beaten
2 tbsp milk
golden syrup, to spoon over
custard, to serve

1 Butter a small microwave-proof pudding basin. In a separate bowl, rub the butter into the flour and baking powder, then stir in the sugar and sultanas. Gradually add the eggs and milk to make a wet cake mixture.

2 Spoon into the basin and make a deep hollow in the centre with the back of the spoon. Cover the basin with cling film, pierce with the tip of a knife and microwave on high for 4½–5 minutes until well risen and firm to the touch.

3 Carefully turn the pud out on to a plate and spoon over a generous amount of syrup. Slice and serve with custard.

PER SERVING (6) 368 kcals, protein 6g, carbs 50g, fat 16g, sat fat 9g, fibre 1g, sugar 26g, salt 0.5g

Baileys banana trifles

Swap the booze for extra toffee sauce if you are making this for children. You could assemble this in one big bowl, if you want a big show-stopping dessert.

TAKES 10 MINUTES • MAKES 6

300ml pot extra-thick double cream
7 tbsp Baileys liqueur
6 chocolate brownies (about 250g/9oz total), broken up, or use crumbled chocolate biscuits or loaf cake
3 bananas, sliced
500g pot vanilla custard
6 tbsp toffee sauce
25g/1oz chocolate, grated

1 Mix the cream with 1 tablespoon of the Baileys and set aside.
2 Divide the brownie pieces, crumbled biscuits or loaf cake among six glasses, then drizzle each with 1 tablespoon of Baileys. Top with the sliced bananas, custard and Baileys cream, dividing equally, then drizzle with toffee sauce and finish with grated chocolate. This can be made a few hours ahead and stored in the fridge.

PER TRIFLE 689 kcals, protein 7g, carbs 63g, fat 46g, sat fat 26g, fibre 2g, sugar 53g, salt 0.43g

Apple & cornflake pots

You could make more of these fruity pots than you need and then enjoy them for breakfast the next day.

TAKES 25 MINUTES ● MAKES 4

800g/1lb 12oz Bramley apples, peeled and sliced
3 tbsp golden caster sugar
2 tbsp golden syrup
25g/1oz butter
85g/3oz cornflakes
200ml/7fl oz low-fat crème fraîche

1 Put the apples, caster sugar and 3 tablespoons water in a pan and cook over a medium heat, stirring occasionally, for 10 minutes until softened. Divide the mixture among four glass tumblers and leave to cool.

2 Meanwhile, heat the golden syrup and butter in a large bowl in the microwave for 1 minute to melt. Add the cornflakes and stir well to coat.

3 Top the cooled apple with the crème fraîche, then divide the cornflake mix among the glasses.

PER POT 372 kcals, protein 4g, carbs 60g, fat 13g, sat fat 8g, fibre 3g, sugar 44g, salt 0.8g

Spiced French toast

If hot cross buns aren't available then this recipe works just as well with tea cakes.

TAKES 15 MINUTES • SERVES 4

4 tbsp soft butter
2 tsp ground cinnamon
2 eggs, beaten
100ml/3½fl oz milk
4 hot cross buns, split in half
vanilla ice cream and maple syrup
   (optional), to serve

1 Mix 3 tablespoons of the butter with half the cinnamon and mash together. Beat together the eggs, milk and remaining cinnamon in a bowl. Sandwich two slices of hot cross bun together with half the cinnamon butter and repeat with the remaining two slices.

2 Dip the buns in the egg mix and leave to soak for a few seconds. Heat the remaining butter in a frying pan until foaming. Cook the hot cross buns for 1–2 minutes each side until light golden (you may need to do this in two batches). Press down on them as you cook. Serve each portion topped with a scoop of ice cream and a drizzle of maple syrup, if you like.

PER SERVING 334 kcals, protein 9g, carbs 33g, fat 20g, sat fat 10g, fibre 1g, sugar 14g, salt 0.44g

Index